SMARTER KIDS

Other books by Lawrence J. Greene

Learning Disabilities and Your Child (1987)

Kids Who Underachieve (1986)

Getting Smarter (1985)

Kids Who Hate School (1984)

SMARTER KIDS

by

Lawrence J. Greene

THE BODY PRESS
PRICE STERN SLOAN, INC.

The Body Press
A division of Price Stern Sloan, Inc.
360 North La Cienega Boulevard
Los Angeles, California 90048

Manufactured in the United States of America

10 9 8 7 6 5 4 3 2

Library of Congress Cataloging-in-Publication Data

Greene, Lawrence J.
  Smarter kids.

  Includes index.
  1. Child rearing.   2. Thought and thinking.
3. Children—Time management.   I. Title.
HQ769.G746   1987   649'.1   87-15824
ISBN 0-89586-547-5

CONTENTS

INTRODUCTION 1

CHAPTER 1—DEVELOPING THE CAPACITY TO THINK 7

CHAPTER 2—APPLYING INTELLIGENCE 32

CHAPTER 3—STRATEGIC INTROSPECTION 64

CHAPTER 4—ESTABLISHING PRIORITIES AND GOALS 94

CHAPTER 5—TIME MANAGEMENT AND
              ORGANIZATIONAL SKILLS 129

CHAPTER 6—LEARNING TO BOUNCE BACK 156

CHAPTER 7—PUTTING IT ALL TOGETHER 180

CHAPTER 8—FOLLOW-UP INVENTORIES 209

INDEX 224

Acknowledgments

I would like to express my gratitude to Dennis Fregger and to Kathryn Welds for their suggestions, incisive criticism, and support.

For Robbie Dunton

You bring out the best in every child whose life you touch. You have been my teacher, too, and I am so grateful for all that you have taught me.

"The living self has one purpose only: to come into its own fullness of being, as a tree comes into full blossom, or a bird into spring beauty, or a tiger into luster."
D. H. Lawrence

Introduction

Tory put his shoulder to the door and pushed. At first, he was surprised that it wouldn't open, but when he finally did shove it open, he discovered that the football gear he had stashed behind it had fallen on the floor. Once in the room, the 13-year-old threw his book bag on his bed which was, as usual, unmade. In fact, the bed hadn't been made since his mother had changed the sheets the previous Saturday.

The seventh-grader began to search through the mass of papers on his desk. His corrected English essay had been due today, but he had forgotten to bring it to school. Even if he had brought it, he would have received a low grade because he had also forgotten to make the corrections. Although Tory hadn't seen the paper for at least 5 days, he dimly remembered putting it on his desk. But then again, perhaps he had put it somewhere else. Tory knew that if he could find the paper under the mess on his desk, he could still hand it in tomorrow. His grade, of course, would be lowered by one letter because the report would be late. That didn't particularly bother him. "Boy, is the teacher a pain," Tory thought angrily as he rifled through the crumpled papers. "She's just like my parents, always hassling me over stupid things. If she sends my folks another deficiency notice, they'll ground me again. Where is that dumb paper!"

Tory's parents no longer entered his room, except once a week when his mom would change the sheets. The arguments about his chronic sloppiness and disorganization had been going on ever since first grade. Finally, his parents had given up and reluctantly resigned themselves to the fact that their son's room would remain a disaster area. From time to time, they would bring up the issues of organization and neatness. A predictable argument would ensue and they would once again wash their hands of the matter.

Despite an IQ of 134 and good academic skills, Tory's grades were in the C- range. His superior intelligence could not compensate for his sloppy work and late assignments.

Accustomed to using only a small portion of his potential ability, Tory accepted the fact that he was an "airhead" when it came to schoolwork and keeping his life organized. Intellectually passive and unmotivated, he submitted to the ritual of being educated because he was required to do so. Doing the minimum possible had become his standard operating procedure. Even his parents' threats of punishment and their periodic outbursts of anger no longer affected him.

Watching a child waste precious potential and make flawed decisions has to be one of parenting's most heart-wrenching ordeals. The parents of a potentially capable child who recognize that their child is not thinking or acting smart cannot help but feel sadness, frustration, stress, and even resentment. The natural inclination is to help. Unfortunately, this desire to intervene frequently misfires and succeeds only in triggering communication breakdowns, arguments and alienation.

Most parents recognize that the world their child will enter upon completing school is competitive and that its lessons can be harsh. Those with children like Tory have justification for concern. They realize that if their child enters the job market with poorly developed thinking and academic skills, he is on a collision course with reality. He is destined to discover that most of society's rewards are reserved for those who use their intellectual resources and have marketable skills.

Let me describe another child. Her name is Lisa. She is 12 years old and attends the same junior high school as Tory. Lisa is certainly not a perfect child. Like any preadolescent, she talks to her friends on the telephone, watches TV, wastes time, acts silly and occasionally misbehaves. Although her IQ is lower than Tory's, her grades are in the A- range. Five primary characteristics distinguish her from Tory:

1. She is enthusiastic about learning.
2. She is goal-oriented.
3. She is organized.
4. She takes pride in her work and her achievements.
5. She thinks strategically.

Unlike Tory, Lisa generally gives 100 percent when she undertakes a project or an assignment. When she studies, she aims for specific grades on her quizzes and exams and for specific grades in her courses. She checks and rechecks her work before submitting it, looking for spelling and grammar mistakes. As she reads her textbooks, she makes a conscious effort to identify important information, and she tries to guess what her teachers will ask on tests.

Lisa is as organized at home as she is in school. She keeps track of her possessions in the same way that she keeps track of her assignments. Although she does not enjoy doing certain chores, she does them with relatively little fussing. Her style is to get unpleasant tasks done as quickly as possible so she has time for things she enjoys.

Lisa's grades in school belie the commonly held belief that intelligence alone determines whether or not a child will achieve in school and in life. This idea goes hand-in-hand with the belief that the capacity of the human brain is determined exclusively by genetics and cannot be altered. Such an argument conjures up images of infants on a production line where each is assigned a number that defines his or her maximum level of achievement.

The contention that genetics exclusively defines a child's level of achievement is, of course, nonsense. Although it is true that children's IQ's are genetically determined, it is certainly *not* true that children must passively resign themselves to the whims of nature. A child is more than a bundle of cells bound together by genetic code!

You have chosen this book because you recognize that if your child is to succeed in an increasingly complex and technological society, he or she must have a competitive edge. From the onset, let me clearly state the basic premise of this book. *You can increase your child's achievement potential by teaching your child specific methods for using his or her inherited intelligence more effectively.* With appropriate training, any child between the ages of 7 and 17 *can* become smarter. This book provides you with a practical, easy-to-apply system for achieving this objective with *your* child.

The second premise of *Smarter Kids* is also simple. *You are your child's primary teacher, and you can and should play a central role in stimulating the development of his or her thinking skills.* This book will teach you how to do so without triggering "showdowns" and "shoot-outs."

The third premise of this book involves basic logic. *The more you understand how your child learns, the more you can contribute to your child's developing intellect. Smarter Kids* will help you acquire this insight.

Contributing to the development of a child's intellect can be one of parenting's most creative and rewarding experiences. Parents and children who make discoveries together create a very special and enduring bond.

"What about the schools? What is their role?" you might be wondering. Helping a child become smarter is, of course, the primary responsibility of our educational system. In theory, our schools teach our children to think analytically. In practice, this does not always happen. Millions of children emerge from high school not knowing how to use their intelligence to solve problems. Although some schools are now formally teaching students how to think and study effectively, countless others provide no special instruction in such vital subjects as study skills and analytical thinking.*

*For more information, see *Getting Smarter* (Lawrence Greene and Leigh Jones-Bamman), David S. Lake Publishers, Belmont, CA, 1985.

Reality dictates that training your child to think smart cannot be the exclusive responsibility of the school system. You must share the responsibility. If you are concerned about the quality of your child's thinking and problem-solving skills, now is the time for you to "step into the ring."

The activities and exercises that follow are designed to improve the quality of your child's reactions to challenges and problems. Your child will learn how to:

1. Think logically
2. Think analytically
3. Think strategically
4. Manage time
5. Establish priorities
6. Establish goals
7. Use goals as a means for solving problems
8. Learn actively
9. Identify important information
10. Remember information by making it relevant
11. Use critical thinking skills to solve problems

To help your child achieve these objectives, you must do more than simply read a book and shake your head affirmatively when you encounter an interesting or thought-provoking idea. If you are to help your child become smarter, you must serve as your child's intellectual guide, and you must commit the necessary time, energy, support, patience and love.

Being a role model is a major responsibility. Knowing that your words and deeds influence your child's attitudes, thoughts, skills and values thrusts you into a position of monumental importance. One fact of life is inescapable: on a conscious and unconscious level, your child is constantly measuring and gauging your responses to life. If you are willing to share your problem-solving skills, your intellectual curiosity and your enthusiasm for learning, you will have a profoundly positive effect on the development of your child's capacity to think.

Before you and your child begin the journey, one final note about the format of this book is in order. *Smarter Kids* is intended to be an interactive book. For your child to derive full value from the smart-thinking methods, you must be willing to work together (i.e., interact) on the checklists, exercises, activities and dialogues. These supplemental materials have been carefully designed to guide your child through a sequential learning process. They also provide the opportunities for practice that are essential to mastery of any new skill.

The objective of *Smarter Kids* is to do more than simply explain how a child might theoretically learn how to think more effectively. Rather, the objective is to *change and enhance your child's thinking behaviors.* Working together is vital to achieving this goal!

In each chapter, you will find checklists, model dialogues and exercises. Before problems can be resolved, they must first be identified. The checklists are designed to help you and your child identify deficit areas. Once these deficits are pinpointed, the next step for you and your child is to examine how his thinking and problem-solving skills might be improved. Effective parent-child communication is essential to this process.

The dialogues model non-threatening communication strategies that can be used to broach and examine issues relevant to developing more effective and efficient thinking skills. Basic logic underlies the tone and format of these dialogues. When parents avoid triggering "knee-jerk" resistance and resentment, they significantly improve the prospects of reorienting their child's self-defeating attitudes and behavior.

The supplemental activities provide additional opportunities for applying, refining and mastering smart-thinking skills. You will note that some of the interactive material is oriented toward younger children and some toward teenagers. The appropriate age range for these sections is clearly indicated. If you are the parent of a teenager, feel free to skip over the material intended for younger children. Conversely, if your child is 9 years old, you may decide not to read the teenage-oriented material at this time.

Serving as your child's intellectual guide offers two additional bonuses. The open, sensitive sharing and examination of thoughts and feelings must inevitably enhance the quality of communication between you and your child. This enhanced communication, in turn, must inevitably improve the quality of your relationship.

An old proverb states that God gives every creature just as much understanding as it needs for its existence. If this proverb is true, as I am convinced it is, then it follows that the child who fails to develop his capacity to understand himself and the events in his world will experience a lower level of existence. As the parents of a potentially capable child, you cannot allow this unnecessary waste of human resources to occur.

SUGGESTIONS FOR USING THIS BOOK EFFECTIVELY

1. Read each chapter entirely before beginning the interactive activities with your child.
2. Consider in advance how you might best present the material.
3. Create a relaxed and cooperative atmosphere.

4. Know when it is time to stop the session. Younger children have a shorter attention span, and teenagers can become resistant if the sessions are too long.
5. Don't insist that your child "get it" the first time you present a concept or new thinking skill. Your child may require several exposures and may need to practice.
6. Vary the style of your interactive sessions. Predictability and repetitiveness cause boredom and resistance.
7. Make the interactive sessions interesting and enjoyable.
8. Avoid judgmental language that triggers resistance and resentment (e.g., "You are thinking irresponsibly.")
9. Be supportive if your child falters.
10. Be sensitive to your child's feelings and vulnerabilities.
11. Acknowledge your child for his efforts.
12. Affirm your child for improvement.
13. Express positive expectations.
14. Above all, *be caring and loving!*

Chapter 1
Developing the Capacity to Think

GETTING FROM POINT A TO POINT B

Jeremy wanted to carry as much as he could on one trip. He didn't have time to make "hundreds" of trips from the car to the campsite. One thousand yards was an endless journey to a 10-year-old when there were forests to explore, creeks to ford and hills to climb. If he could carry the sleeping bags, his knapsack, the charcoal, the charcoal starter and the canteens in one trip, he would have done what his dad had told him to do.

As he began to load up, he realized that he couldn't possibly carry everything. He didn't have enough hands. In the back of the trunk, he could see the corner of the piece of canvas cloth that his dad used to cover the ground under the sleeping bags. He grabbed the canvas, dumped the gear in it, pulled the ends together into a bundle, and wrestled the bundle over his right shoulder. Lopsided and shaky from the weight, he somehow managed to stumble to the campsite. He was free!

ANALYTICAL THINKING

Carrying a pile of camping gear from the car to the campsite in one trip may not appear to be particularly brilliant. "Isn't any child of average intelligence capable of figuring this out?" you might be thinking. The answer is "yes," of course. But it is a qualified "yes." Believe it or not, many children of average to superior intelligence would have difficulty with this basic logistical problem and might end up making two or three trips instead of one.

At first glance, figuring out that it is efficient to transport camping gear by wrapping it in a piece of canvas and throwing the bundle over your shoulder would seem to involve rudimentary thinking skills. Jeremy's solution, however, was actually the end-product of a relatively complex analytical process. Although he was not consciously aware of this process, he was keenly aware of his objective: to get the camping equipment to the campsite as quickly as possible. Realizing that the standard load-up-your-arms approach would require too many trips and too much time, Jeremy devised a clever alternative strategy. As his brain sorted out the data and sought a solution to the problem, it followed a classic problem-solving progression:

1. I don't have enough hands.
2. What can I do to help myself?
3. There's a piece of canvas. I can use it.
4. Let's see if everything fits when I make a bundle.
5. Now what am I going to do with the bundle?
6. I'll try it over my shoulder. If that doesn't work, maybe I can drag it.
7. It works! I can make it in one trip, assuming I don't fall and break my neck.

The first step in Jeremy's analysis was to assess the situation. He had to identify the objective, consider the conditions, examine his options, and reorient his thinking from the traditional way of carrying things. In deriving his solution, he may have drawn upon his own past experience with bundles, or he may have associated his current problem with similar problems he had seen someone else solve.

As Jeremy proceeded through the steps of the problem analysis, he drew upon his innate intelligence. Had he possessed a low IQ, he might have struggled through a protracted process of trial and error and might have never solved the problem efficiently. Jeremy's solution, however, required more than basic intelligence. It also required basic smartness. By thinking analytically, the child was able to figure out how to get the job done with a minimum amount of grief and wasted effort. This "finding the shortest line between two points" is the essence of smart thinking. Seeing the piece of canvas was the catalyst. Once he began the analytical process, the 10-year-old was able to perform the subsequent mental functions almost instantaneously.

DISTINGUISHING INTELLIGENCE FROM SMARTNESS

A vital distinction must be made between smartness and intelligence. Although the two phenomena often overlap, each can operate independently. One child, for example, may be so intelligent that he can solve calculus problems in fifth grade. The same child, however, may not be particularly smart and may have had two bicycles stolen because he forgot to lock them in the school bike rack. Another child may be smart enough to avoid getting into a fight with the class bully, but not sufficiently intelligent to win a scholarship to college.

Intelligence may be defined as the capacity to think creatively, to recognize similarities and differences, to analyze information, to solve problems, to associate past experiences with current experiences, to learn from mistakes, to understand abstract ideas, and to distill information.

When faced with an intellectually challenging problem, the intelligent child systematically analyzes the situation and asks himself some or all of the following questions:

1. Is this problem similar to one I have already solved?
2. What are the similarities and differences?
3. How did I solve the similar problem?
4. This factor in the problem is different. How could this change affect the solution?
5. I made this mistake once before. How could I avoid making it again?

To be intelligent, a child does not necessarily have to ask these questions on a conscious level. The process can become so natural and ingrained that it happens without the child even being aware of the fact that he has gone through a systematic, problem-solving process.

Although smartness and intelligence are linked, smartness primarily involves the practical application of intelligence.

Smartness may be defined as the capacity to apply intelligence, to get from point A to point B efficiently, to calculate the odds, to plan strategically, to understand cause and effect, to bounce back from defeat, to neutralize obstacles, and to survive in a competitive world.

When faced with a challenge or a problem, the child who thinks smart asks himself the following questions:

1. What do I want to achieve?
2. How can I get the job done successfully?
3. How can I avoid time-consuming and energy-consuming mistakes?
4. How can I reduce the odds of failure?

Jeremy's solution to the problem of transporting the camping gear illustrates the role of smartness in solving life's basic problems. The steps involved in smart thinking are sequential, but as has been noted above, a child need not be consciously aware of the steps. In fact, if someone were to ask Jeremy how he came up with the solution, he would probably respond: "I don't know. I just did."

Although a child can be expected to confront a wide range of challenges and problems during his lifetime, the procedure he must use to resolve these problems and challenges successfully involves key common denominators. These common denominators are the building blocks of smart thinking, and they are as relevant and applicable in math class as they are on a camping trip or on the football field.

BUILDING BLOCKS OF SMART THINKING

1. *Collect the data.* These things need to be carried in one trip to the campsite which is 1000 yards away.
2. *Compare the data with what is already known.* What are the possible ways I might use to carry all this equipment in one trip?
3. *Figure out what to do with the data.* Given the size and weight of the equipment, how can I organize it so that it is transportable?
4. *Figure out what can be done to get the job done.* This piece of canvas can be used to create a bundle that I can carry or drag to the campsite .
5. *Check the hypothesis.* All the equipment fits into the bundle, and I can carry it over my shoulder.

A brilliant child might run through these steps very quickly and might even skip a step or two. Despite this shortcut, the child's analytical process would be essentially the same.

Because our brains are continually solving "simple" problems and usually zip through the required steps rapidly and efficiently, we tend to be somewhat cavalier about the many services the brain provides. Like our car, we assume that it will be there to serve us when we need it.

To solve his problem, a child must be able to focus his intelligence and plan strategically. Unfortunately, not all children develop this capacity. Even the highly intelligent child may not be especially smart in school. He might, for instance, lose important papers or forget to do assignments. He may write a brilliant essay but fail to write legibly or proofread the essay. For many potentially capable children, the bridge connecting their intelligence quotient and their smartness quotient is often up.

10

Some children seem to acquire the ability to think smart by a natural osmosis process. These children do not need a great deal of direct help from their parents. Others, who are equally bright and potentially capable, never learn how to develop or refine their intellectual resources without systematic adult guidance.

A child *inherits his intelligence,* but he *acquires his smartness.* This acquisition process is profoundly influenced by the child's environment. Children who are encouraged—or required by necessity—to think analytically generally become smart. Conversely, those who are permitted to float through life intellectually anesthetized become habituated to passive thinking and rarely become smart.

DEVELOPING YOUR CHILD'S BRAIN POWER

The brain of a newborn infant might be compared to a dry, tightly compressed sponge. To the casual observer, a dry sponge might not appear particularly impressive. Its seeming simplicity is misleading, however, for the sponge is remarkably functional. When provided with moisture, a magical transformation occurs. The sponge begins to expand and becomes supple. As the liquid is absorbed, thousands of resilient chambers literally spring to life. Although each individual chamber is useless, collectively the chambers are highly utilitarian.

A child's brain is infinitely more complex than a sponge's primitive system of interactive chambers, but there is one striking parallel. The brain also consists of cells bound together in a system that becomes highly functional when provided with essential nutrients. If deprived of these nutrients, the brain—like the dry sponge—never fully develops its capacity to perform its inherent functions.

As a child's brain passes through natural, preprogrammed developmental stages, it becomes increasingly efficient and potent. Almost from the moment of birth, the infant begins a never-ending process of classifying experiences, committing these experiences to memory, and associating past experiences with present experiences.

Psychologists and educators have documented that a child's intellectual development follows a predictable timetable. Given proper stimulation and adequate instruction, the child's ability to produce spoken and written language and to understand and manipulate numbers will ultimately evolve into the ability to write research papers and to solve algebraic equations. As the brain teaches itself, and is formally trained, its intellectual capabilities expand. If the child possesses normal intelligence and experi-

11

ences no significant emotional or environmental traumas, this expansion will ultimately permit him to perform the higher level mental functions necessary for survival and achievement in a complex, competitive society. The training process that makes this possible is called *education*. The brain's response to this training process is called *learning*.

The child's compelling need to learn and develop his intellect is imprinted by nature. Although controlled to a large extent by genetic code, the learning process is actually quite fragile and tenuous. Simply inheriting potential ability and receiving formal education does not ensure that a child will become capable of efficient thought, strategic planning and goal-directed effort. The child's brain must be stimulated and nurtured, or it may never become fully functional.

SURVIVAL SKILLS

Most of us take our brain's resources for granted. The trained, confident, competent electrician has little doubt that he will be able to install a new circuit board, and the trained, confident, competent surgeon has little doubt that he can perform the gastrectomy that will eliminate a patient's ulcer.

It is only when our brain does not work properly that we begin to appreciate how well it serves us. Sometimes the breakdown is caused by temporary conditions such as drowsiness or depression. More serious obstacles to problem-solving could involve low intelligence, low aptitude or deficient skills. For example, we may find ourselves struggling to solve a complicated algebraic equation, to understand the instructions for setting up a computer, or to comprehend the symbolism of a beautiful poem. As we slam against these barriers, we become more acutely aware of our limitations.

During a typical day, a child confronts countless major and minor problems that he must solve. Can he find enough kids to play baseball after school? Can she convince her parents to let her spend the night at her friend's house? Can he find someone to lend him yesterday's biology notes? Can she figure out how to improve her grade in history? In one way or another, children usually find solutions to most of their problems. The quality of these solutions, however, can vary significantly and is directly linked to the quality of their ability to think smart.

The capacity to analyze and solve problems has always been essential to survival. In prehistoric times, parents realized that if their children were to survive, they would have to teach them how to use a rock as a weapon to kill predators and prey. The thrust of these lessons was quite basic: "Watch me, Son. You stand up here on this ledge when you are throwing a rock at a saber-toothed tiger or a mammoth. If you don't kill him, run!"

Throughout the ages parents have been teaching their children how to survive in a world that can be very cruel to those who function inadequately. They have taught them how to plant and till the soil, how to sew, how to milk cows, how to ride and break horses, how to put on screen windows, and how to do addition and subtraction problems. Through word and deed, parents have also modeled for their children how to respond in social situations, how to negotiate, how to defend themselves, and how to make ethical and moral judgments.

The classic role of parent/teacher is one of the enduring traditions of civilized society. Parents have always functioned as their children's primary teachers. Only during the last 200 years have schools assumed much of the responsibility for training children's minds and teaching survival skills. Despite the fact that teachers in modern society are assigned the job of formally cultivating children's intellectual potential, much of the tilling and fertilization must take place at home. Unfortunately, this family-based intellectual cultivation process does not always occur.

Our society has undergone dramatic changes in the last 25 years. Divorce is epidemic. In many families, both parents have become wage-earners. Professional child care and latchkey children are becoming the rule rather than the exception. Television and videos consume more and more of our children's time.

The transition from a society comprised primarily of tightly knit families to one increasingly comprised of fragmented families has taken its toll. Many parents have less time and inclination to serve as their children's mentors. The tradition of discussing the day's events around the dinner table and reading bedtime stories has been replaced by the tradition of watching TV. Time once allocated to shared activities is now often devoted either to personal pursuits or to mass-media entertainment. Preoccupied with their own lives, aspirations, and problems, many parents have abandoned the custom of sharing their wisdom and teaching their skills to their children. Farmers, of course, realize that poorly cultivated soil produces blighted crops. The application of this basic cause-and-effect axiom to the nuclear family, however, has been largely disregarded.

The evolution of 20th-century society has created a new range of challenges that demand a unique spectrum of skills. For a child to achieve in an increasingly technological world, he must be able to solve problems that are far more complex than those faced by his parents. Children must know how to use computers, how to analyze complicated data, how to develop and implement complex programs, how to manage people and machines, and how to negotiate and sell highly technical equipment and services. Those children who do not acquire these skills and do not develop their intellectual resources are in danger of becoming underachievers.

LEARNING HOW TO LEARN

Learning begins at the moment of birth. Infants quickly figure out how to get responses from their mothers and fathers. Toddlers discover how to propel themselves from here to there and how to open a drawer or a door. First-graders figure out how to decode written symbols that comprise words and how to compute written symbols that comprise numbers. Fourth-graders learn how to remember spelling words, and tenth-graders learn how to remember the phyla in biology.

As children progress through school, the intellectual demands on them increase exponentially. Many parents and teachers assume that at the appropriate time a child will be ready to write a book report or study effectively for a history final. This expectation reflects a basic assumption that children will naturally discover an effective means for getting the job done.

Some children do discover how to work and learn efficiently with little formal instruction. These children teach themselves to read and write and effortlessly master the skills for producing well-crafted essays. When it is time to learn fractions, they do so with little or no difficulty. Such children also intuitively develop an effective system for studying, and learn how to identify, comprehend and remember important information. Identified by our educational system as gifted learners, these "natural" students usually end up at the best universities and colleges.

But what of the other potentially capable children who do not learn effortlessly? What about the child of average or superior intelligence who is not a gifted, natural learner? Can parents do anything to help such a child work up to his potential? Can they motivate him to develop his potential ability? The answer to these last two questions is a resounding *YES!*

CAUSE AND EFFECT

Although they may be bright, and even brilliant, many children never learn how to shift their brains out of cerebral neutral. Knowing *when* to push in the clutch and *how* to run through the gears requires not only skill, it also requires practice.

14

To help the child who is stuck cerebrally, parents must do something that athletic coaches are continually advocating. *They must go back to the basics.* Helping a child understand how his actions and decisions produce predictable reactions is central to this retraining process. The following dialogue models a communication strategy that might be used with children in second grade through tenth grade to help them comprehend the basic logic that links their actions (cause) with the consequences of those actions (effect). This phenomenon is the foundation upon which critical thinking skills rest.

In the dialogue, a parent is talking with a 10-year-old about a bicycle. Please note that it is always advisable to use examples and analogies that relate to your child's interests and life experiences. A second dialogue specifically directed toward teenagers that underscores cause and effect can be found later in this chapter.

The precise words used in this dialogue are not particularly important. What is important is the *style* and *tone* of the parent-child interaction. If the dialogue is not appropriate or relevant for your child, choose a subject that is. Use your own words, and do not lose sight of the objective of the dialogue—to model a method of communicating that stimulates your child's awareness of the consequences of his or her choices and actions.

GUIDELINES FOR EFFECTIVE COMMUNICATION WITH CHILDREN

1. *Consider your objectives.*

    Do you want to change your child's behavior (e.g., a neater room)?

    Do you want your child to commit himself to a particular course of action?

    Do you want compliance with your wishes?

    Do you want collaboration on a particular project?

2. *Make the subject as engaging and interesting as possible.*

    How can you modify your own behavior and style to encourage active involvement in the issues being explored?

    How can you use examples and analogies that your child can understand and appreciate?

3. *Communicate optimism and positive expectations.*

    Can you avoid being judgmental? ("You certainly don't care very much about the feelings of others.")

Can you avoid labeling? ("You're being irresponsible!")

Can you avoid appearing rigid or arbitrary? ("The answer is 'no', period and end of discussion!")

Can you avoid blaming? ("You're always creating tension at the dinner table.")

4. *Establish specific behavioral goals.*

What changes and/or objectives would you ideally like your child to achieve?

Can you help your child appreciate the value of these changes and/or objectives?

Can you figure out how to motivate your child to want to make these changes and achieve these objectives?

5. *Listen actively.*

Can you identify multiple levels of meaning? ("I hate my teacher?" could mean "I'm too dumb to be able to please my teacher.")

Can you distinguish between facts, rationalizations and excuses?

6. *Set the stage.*

Can you establish a context that encourages cooperation and mutual respect? (Examples of ways to broach a discussion of issues might include: "I'd like to discuss something with you that I find interesting and I think you will also find interesting." "Let's examine an interesting situation together." "I'm reading a book about developing kid's thinking skills. Would you be willing to work with me on some of the activities?")

Model Dialogue #1
CAUSE AND EFFECT
Children ages 7-12

Parent: You just received a new bike for Christmas. It was the one you asked for, and I know that you realize it was expensive. Let me ask you a question. If you wanted to meet your friend Sean at Tony's Pizza Pub and play the video games, would you park your new bike in front of the store without locking it?

16

Child:	No.
Parent:	Could you tell me why?
Child:	Because it might get stolen.
Parent:	Right. Because your bike is important, you would want to lock it.
Child:	Yeah!
Parent:	Let's assume you lock your bike by placing a chain through the tire and wrapping the chain around the frame. You then go inside to play the video games. You come out 30 minutes later and discover your bike is gone. What would you do then?
Child:	I'd go look for it.
Parent:	That certainly makes sense. OK. You wander around the neighborhood looking for your bike, but you can't find it. What next?
Child:	I'd call Mom.
Parent:	All right. What would she do?
Child:	She'd come with the car and help me look for the bike.
Parent:	Would she do anything else?
Child:	She'd call the police.
Parent:	That makes sense. Nevertheless, the bike is stolen and no one can find it. Why do you think it was stolen?
Child:	I didn't lock it to something.
Parent:	Like a pole or a sign post?
Child:	Yeah.
Parent:	Unfortunately, the bike is gone and probably won't be found. What's next?
Child:	What do you mean?
Parent:	Do you want another bike?
Child:	Yes.
Parent:	Do you think I would buy you another one?
Child:	No.
Parent:	Tell me why I wouldn't buy you another one.

Child: You'd be mad at me.

Parent: And?

Child: I was dumb not to lock it to a pole or something.

Parent: Let's say I made a deal with you. I offered to pay half the cost of a new bike if you would work for the other half. Would you be willing?

Child: Yeah.

Parent: How could you earn the money?

Child: I could mow lawns. Or I could deliver newspapers.

Parent: You'd have to work hard for the money. You'd have to get up at 5:30 in the morning. During the winter it would be dark and cold, and you would have to get yourself up before anyone else in the house. Would it be worth it if you could have another bike?

Child: Yes.

Parent: Let's say you got your new bike and Sean wanted to meet you again to play video games. What would you do?

Child: I could walk there.

Parent: Or?

Child: I could ask Mom to drive me.

Parent: Or?

Child: I could ride my bike and when I got there I could lock it to something.

Parent: Let's say you left your bike in front and didn't lock it to something. Would that be smart or dumb?

Child: Dumb!

Parent: And if you did lock it to something, would that be smart or dumb?

Child: Smart!

Parent: Good. You got the point. I know that you are smart, and I expect smart things from you. OK?

Child: OK.

Parent: Thanks for discussing this with me. You can go play now.

18

You will note that in the preceding dialogue the parent does not lecture his child about the importance of locking his bike. The objective of the session is to help the child develop a heightened awareness of cause and effect *before* his bike is stolen. Had the child's bike already been stolen, the dialogue could have also functioned as a non-punitive means for examining important issues related to responsibility.

This dialogue is intended to demonstrate a method that encourages children to think strategically. When you attempt to use this and other dialogues modeled in this book, you will undoubtedly discover that your own child's responses are different from the hypothetical responses in the dialogues. For this reason, you must be prepared to adapt your language and adjust your reactions accordingly. Ideally, the discussion will evolve and assume its own momentum. The exact words you use are unimportant. What is important is that you not fall into the trap of delivering lectures or sermons to your child about the value of thinking analytically. Periodically remind yourself that your basic objectives are to help your child develop the ability to:

1. Think about the consequences of his or her actions.
2. Analyze events.
3. Draw logical conclusions.
4. Apply his or her intelligence in the process of finding solutions to problems.

When you help your child acquire these skills and habits, you are helping him establish a solid foundation for smart thinking.

DETERMINING IF YOUR CHILD HAS DIFFICULTY WITH CAUSE AND EFFECT

Children who do not link cause and effect are on shaky ground. Unaware of the potential effect of their actions, they tend to act without thinking. This lack of reality awareness can seriously undermine their ability to achieve.

Smart children plan. They think about what they need to do and how to do it. Not-so-smart children seldom plan and seldom think strategically. They are oblivious to the consequences of their actions (or lack of action), and as a consequence, rarely develop their full Smartness Quotient.

One of the primary characteristics of focused intelligence (i.e., smartness) is the capacity to learn from life experiences. A smart child needs to fall off a skateboard with a loose wheel only once to realize that he doesn't want to do so again. The child who repeatedly falls off the skateboard because he doesn't take the time to fix the wheel is obviously not thinking smart.

The following checklist will help you determine if your child understands cause and effect and if your child appreciates its effect on his or her life.

Checklist for Parent
CAUSE AND EFFECT

Code: 0 = Never   1 = Rarely
       2 = Sometimes   3 = Often   4 = Always

My child leaves projects and assignments until the last minute.   _____

My child does not allow sufficient time to complete projects.   _____

My child is disorganized.   _____

My child acts impulsively and without thinking.   _____

My child is chronically forgetful.   _____

My child repeats the same mistakes.   _____

My child resists assistance.   _____

My child rarely establishes short-term or long-term goals.   _____

My child has little sense of purpose.   _____

My child gives up easily.   _____

My child avoids responsibility.   _____

My child tends to blame others for his or her problems.   _____

My child is not especially concerned about potential danger or risk.   _____

My child appears satisfied to do a second-rate job.   _____

20

Interpreting the Checklist

A pattern of 3's and 4's in the answers to the statements on this checklist suggests that your child needs assistance in understanding cause and effect. If you uncover such a pattern, you are urged to initiate discussions—such as the one modeled in Dialogue #1—that reinforce an awareness of the consequences of one's actions. It bears re-emphasizing that these discussions should not be lectures or sermons! Specific activities designed to heighten this awareness are found at the end of this chapter. A similar cause-and-effect dialogue oriented toward teenagers can be found below.

COMMUNICATING WITH TEENAGERS

As most parents of teenagers can attest, attempts to change a child's behavior or _modus operandi_ can elicit a great deal of resistance. This is especially true when teenagers feel that their parents are using them to try out a new parenting technique that they just discovered in some magazine or book.

It is a natural human trait to become habituated to the status quo, even if this status quo is stressful or unpleasant. It is also common for teenagers to be convinced that their parents do not have the answers and could not possibly understand their feelings and concerns. For this reason, presenting the material and introducing the systems suggested in this book require that parents think strategically.

Before proceeding, it might be a good idea to review the different types of interactive activities you will find in this book.

★ _Checklists:_ Some of the checklists are designed to be completed by parents, and others are intended for children to complete. Their purpose is to pinpoint deficit areas that should be examined.

★ _Model Dialogues:_ These hypothetical discussions between parents and children are intended to demonstrate how issues might be productively explored in a constructive, non-emotionally charged context.

★ _Supplemental Activities:_ These exercises are intended to provide practice in problem-solving. They also reinforce the concepts and issues that are being examined in each chapter. The additional practice is designed for both skill mastery and confidence.

21

As you present the different activities, the following guidelines are recommended in addition to the basic communication guidelines discussed on page 15.

ADDITIONAL GUIDELINES FOR INTERACTING WITH YOUR CHILD

(See page 15 for basic communication guidelines.)

1. *Create a non-stressful atmosphere.* Whenever possible, weave the methods and dialogues into casual conversation. Although a special meeting or "summit conference" can be appropriate and effective, a less formal interaction may produce less resistance. Use your discretion.
2. *Beware of presenting the material in an artificial or stilted manner.* Examine the dialogues and methods carefully before attempting to use them. Adapt them to your own style and adjust the vocabulary so that it "feels right." Visualize and hear yourself communicating successfully with your child and using the material comfortably.
3. *Avoid giving the appearance that the dialogues and problem-solving methods follow a predicable formula.*
   Kids are very perceptive, even younger children. If they conclude that you have become a "machine," they will respond by resisting and even mocking your efforts. Choose the moment to introduce the material carefully. Permit your child to modify the methods to suit her needs and personality. Although you want your child to learn a practical system for analyzing and resolving problems, you do not want her to think the system is chiseled in stone.
4. *Be honest.* Tell your child that you would like to work together with her on developing problem-solving skills and communication skills. Let your child know that there will probably be some false starts and that you want feedback. Also let your child know that you are committed to using the methods for a trial period and that there will be a time for reassessment. Assure your child that she will participate in this reassessment process.
5. *Be patient.* New attitudes are rarely learned in one day!
6. *Be supportive.* A child who is asked to examine and change behaviors and attitudes will usually run into some roadblocks and take some detours. At these times, your child especially needs your love, your support, and your faith in his ability to prevail.

7. *Be creative.* If your child is not responding to your efforts to engage him in a discussion, see if you can figure out how to involve him and defuse his resistance. Try to figure out why your child is resistant. Is his behavior caused by anger, sensitivity or insecurity? Is he confused by your attempts to change the "game-plan" and relate to him in a different way? Or is he simply anxious to do something else at the time?

8. *"Read" the situation and back off if the session has gone too long or if your child is responding negatively.* You can always broach the subject again at a more opportune time. In the interim, you can assess the situation and devise a more effective strategy for presenting the material.

Model Dialogue #2
CAUSE AND EFFECT
Teenagers ages 13-17

Parent: I'm curious about how you might respond to this situation. You hear about a party that is being held at someone's house on Saturday night. You know the kid, but he's not a friend. You and your buddies go to the party and discover that the boy's parents are away for the weekend. Have you ever been to such a party?

Teenager: Yeah.

Parent: OK. Some of the kids start drinking beer. Tell me your reaction to this.

Teenager: Kids drink beer at parties.

Parent: I realize that. The fact that they do doesn't particularly please me, but let's not deal with this issue now. You're at the party. You decide to drink beer, or not to drink beer. What are the reasons for your decision to drink it or not to drink it?

Teenager: If everybody's doing it, the cool thing would be to drink beer.

Parent: Okay. What other reasons?

Teenager: I like the taste of beer. When kids drink beer, they have more fun.

23

Parent:	And?
Teenager:	That's all.
Parent:	What might be your reasons for not drinking beer?
Teenager:	It's illegal.
Parent:	And?
Teenager:	I could get in trouble if the police bust the party.
Parent:	Is it possible that you might also be held responsible if any damage was done to the house or the property?
Teenager:	Yeah, I guess.
Parent:	What would happen if some of your friends go out and end up on the front lawn drinking. Let's assume the music from inside is very loud, and the kids outside start to make a lot of noise. Tell me what your reaction would be to this situation.
Teenager:	I don't know.
Parent:	Would you go onto the lawn with your friends?
Teenager:	I might.
Parent:	What possible things could happen?
Teenager:	The police might come.
Parent:	Yes. What are the consequences?
Teenager:	We could get in trouble.
Parent:	I assume you know it's against the law to serve liquor to minors and to drink on the street. Why do you think this law exists?
Teenager:	Kids get drunk, act crazy, and then drive their cars.
Parent:	How do you think the police would react if a neighbor complained that kids were drinking and making a lot of noise?
Teenager:	They'd be mad.
Parent:	They would probably want to talk to the owners of the house, wouldn't they? But the owners are away for the weekend. What do you think they would do then?
Teenager:	They would tell us to stop.
Parent:	Do you think they might even arrest some of the kids if they were drunk and neighbors complained?

Teenager:	Maybe.
Parent:	Do you think they have the right to arrest all of the kids who are drinking?
Teenager:	Yes, I guess so.
Parent:	Do you think the chances of getting arrested increase if you or one of your friends talks back to the officers or acts like a wise guy?
Teenager:	Yes.
Parent:	What do you think would happen to you if you were arrested.
Teenager:	They'd take me to the police station.
Parent:	And they'd book you?
Teenager:	Probably.
Parent:	Fingerprint you? Take your picture and maybe even a strip search?
Teenager:	Yeah, I guess.
Parent:	Do you think they might lock you up until we arrived?
Teenager:	Yeah.
Parent:	Tell me what else would probably happen.
Teenager:	You and Mom would be mad. And you'd ground me.
Parent:	Do you think you would have to appear in juvenile court? Would we need to get you a lawyer?
Teenager:	Yes.
Parent:	Is it possible that the judge might sentence you to juvenile hall?
Teenager:	Yes.
Parent:	Is it possible that you might lose your part-time job when your boss found out?
Teenager:	Yes.
Parent:	And what about your teachers? Would they find out?
Teenager:	Yes.
Parent:	Could that influence their attitudes about you if you ask them to write letters of recommendation to college?

Teenager: Probably.

Parent: All right, enough said. Could the point of all this be that you need to think about the consequences of your choices?

Teenager: Yes.

Parent: I know that you have a good head on your shoulders. You are smart enough and mature enough to make the right decision. You can choose to drink beer illegally, or you can choose not to drink beer illegally. You can choose to go out on the lawn while people are drinking beer illegally, or you can choose not to go out on the lawn. I can't be there to advise you about each of the choices you must make each day. These decisions, however, can profoundly affect your life. When you were younger, you thought that Mom and I were the most powerful people in the world. If anything bad happened, we could always fix it. All little children think their parents can always help them get out of a jam. Well, now that you are becoming an adult, you need to realize that I can't protect you from the police or the court. I don't have that kind of power. You have to decide whether to be smart or dumb. Please think about this. I appreciate our discussion, and I enjoy being able to talk openly about these issues with you.

You will note that the parent does not lecture his son about drinking beer. Nor does he bring up the ethical issue of kids holding parties while their parents are out of town. Although both of these issues are important and should be explored at another time, they are not the focus of this particular discussion. The parent's objective is to help the teenager become more aware of the consequences of his choices. Had he attempted to deliver a sermon, a showdown would have probably ensued, and the teenager would have probably felt compelled to argue, resist or tune out. When pushed to the wall, the natural tendency is to fight or assume a defensive posture. The parent is careful not to belabor the points made during the discussion and allows his son time to think about and "digest" the issues.

Becoming smarter is a process. Changes in behavior and attitude do not occur overnight. One of a parent's primary responsibilities is to provide a catalyst for introspection and analytical problem-solving. By actively involving your child in the process of thinking smart, you create an opportunity for him to acquire insight and to grow intellectually and emotionally.

(Introspection will be examined in depth in Chapter 3.)

Once you have explored the phenomenon of cause and effect with your child, you will need to reinforce your child's awareness of the concept. For instance, when you observe your child acting irresponsibly (e.g., not preparing for an exam or taking unreasonable risks on his skateboard), you might simply ask, "What are the possible consequences of this action?" You could then diplomatically initiate a discussion that examines the underlying issues and the implications. Sometimes a simple and succinct reminder about cause and effect is sufficient.

At the end of this chapter you will find supplemental activities designed to reinforce the concept of cause and effect. Some children may experience difficulty with these activities because they may have trouble expressing themselves or may feel nervous and/or self-conscious. If your child does have difficulty, you must make a special effort to sensitize yourself to his or her response patterns and you must tread lightly in your child's areas of emotional vulnerability. The timid, non-communicative or insecure child will need extra encouragement. "Brainstorming" responses can significantly reduce such a child's anxiety. To help your child become smart, you must do everything in your power to make your child feel smart!

Non-logical answers should be examined with sensitivity. Try to understand your child's thinking process. As he responds to the questions, his deficiencies in reasoning should be mentally noted and might be explored later. It is essential that you do not inadvertently make your child feel dumb or inadequate because his logic is faulty. The purpose for the discussions is to develop and improve your child's reasoning powers. If he concludes that you are highly critical and finds the examination process demeaning, he will probably protect himself by shutting down.

Although the supplemental activities are intended to be instructional, they are also intended to be _fun._ If you make the activities an ordeal, you defeat their purpose. Any inclination to assume the role of a stern, demanding teacher should be resisted!

Supplemental Activity
CAUSE AND EFFECT
Children ages 8-12

Parent: Let's try a game that makes you think about what happens when you decide to do something. I'll tell you the _cause_ of a situation, and you try to figure out what will happen. This is the _effect_ (or consequence).

1. I forget to turn the headlights out in the car, and they are on all night. What happens?
2. I lock my keys in the car.
3. You forget to bring your homework to school.
4. You leave your ice skates at the ice rink.
5. I am continually late for work.
6. You forget to study for a social studies test.
7. It's summer time, and I forget to bring in the ice cream from the car.
8. Your friend decides to steal something from the supermarket.
9. A child throws a pebble at a moving car.
10. You are assigned math homework and you forget to bring home your math textbook.
11. I forget to take my wallet with me when I go to the store.
12. You continually come to soccer practice late.
13. You ride your bike at night without a light.
14. A child tells lies to his parents.
15. You eat too much cake and drink too many soft drinks at a birthday party.

Parent: All of the things I described are called the _____ Good! All of the results are called the _____? Good! This time I tell you the effect and let's see if you can tell me the cause.

1. The car engine stops while we are driving on the highway.
2. You get a bad grade on your science test.
3. The water in the car radiator freezes up.
4. The kitchen sink overflows.
5. You get an A in spelling.
6. Your brother gets into a fight with his best friend.
7. The teacher yells at you in class.
8. We don't have enough milk in the refrigerator.
9. Your Mom is upset with you when she looks in your room.
10. You don't finish your book report on time.
11. Your portable radio stops working.
12. You don't know what your homework assignment is.
13. I can't find my umbrella.
14. You miss the school bus.
15. You forget to study your spelling words.

Parent: Now let's try your giving me a situation and asking me what the consequence would be. Then, we'll try your giving me the consequence and my telling you the cause.

Parent: Now that you understand cause and effect, I want you to think about this every day when you make decisions and choices. Smart kids like you always think about the consequences of their decisions.

Supplemental Activity
CAUSE AND EFFECT
Teenagers ages 13-17

Parent: I'd like to do an activity with you that points out cause and effect. By this I mean that when we do something, we can count on a consequence for our actions. I'll make a statement, and you tell me what you think the effect or result would be.

1. I forget to turn off the lights in the car one night.
2. You cut football practice three times in one week.
3. You don't make it home by curfew time.
4. I forget to pay the electric bill.
5. You don't study for your history midterm.
6. You don't hand in your book report on time.
7. Your best friend spreads untrue rumors about you.
8. Mom forgets to take the registration to the car with her, and she gets stopped by a police officer.
9. You leave food in your room for several days.
10. A friend gets stopped for driving without a license.
11. You forget to write down your science assignment.
12. I get angry at my boss and tell her off.
13. You act up in English class.
14. You cheat on a Spanish test.
15. You leave your portable stereo in the park.

Parent: Now, let's turn the table. I'll give you a consequence, and you figure out the cause.

1. Your mom gets stopped on the highway by a policeman.
2. You get sent to the principal's office by your social studies teacher.
3. You get an A in science.
4. I get a raise at work.
5. You make the tennis team.
6. You are grounded.
7. You get accepted at the college of your choice.
8. You have enough money to buy a car.
9. You become one of the best swimmers on the team.
10. Your brother complains to us, and you get in trouble.
11. You lose your new coat.
12. You get into a fight with your best friend.
13. You get a good summer job.

Parent: Let's turn the tables again. This time you give me some causes, and I'll tell you what I think the effects are.

Parent: Now, you tell me the effect or consequence, and I'll tell you the cause.

[Parents and children should continue the process of linking cause and effect until the concept has been mastered.]

WORKING WITH YOUR CHILD

If you make the time spent doing the activities with your child enjoyable and creative, you will significantly increase your child's receptivity. Learning is far more effective when a child actively participates in the process. Under your guidance, your child will make two important discoveries: thinking smart can be fun, and thinking smart can make life easier.

The tone you create for these interactive sessions can have a dramatic effect on whether or not your child incorporates and applies the smart thinking methods presented in this book. A word of caution is in order. You may try a dialogue similar to the ones modeled in this book and may discover that it doesn't work. If your child does not respond like the hypothetical child in the dialogue, don't become discouraged. You may have to adjust your style if your child is too sophisticated or too immature for the approach. Figure out what works and what doesn't work.

Long discussions may not be necessary to stimulate your child's thinking. For example, your child may state that he has no homework, and you may suspect that he is either deluding himself or attempting to mislead

30

you. Rather than launch into a dialogue, you might simply say, "What are the consequences of getting a poor grade in this course?" The discussion may evolve, or your child may respond, "Don't worry, I'll do OK." If he does respond in this way, you could then reply, "Nevertheless, tell me what the consequences might be if you did do poorly." Or you might say, "I want you to think about the consequences. Let's keep a close watch on how you are doing so we can head off problems before they get out of hand." At this point, the matter could be dropped temporarily. Your child may need some time to think about the issue and the implications of his decision not to study. It is also possible that he truly does not have homework, and you may need to give him the benefit of the doubt until there is evidence to the contrary. As you learn from false starts and refine your ability to "read" the situation and your child, your communication will inevitably improve.

Chapter 2
Applying Intelligence

BEING SMART ENOUGH TO FIND YOUR CAR

The man was angry and exasperated as he wandered amidst the acres of cars in the long-term parking lot at the airport. Exhausted by carrying his suitcases and furious with himself for not having written down the number of the section where he had parked his car 10 days earlier, he left his luggage near a lamp post. He was so upset that he no longer cared if his bags were stolen. It would serve him right for being so stupid. It was 3 a.m., and what had been a wonderful Caribbean vacation was ending horribly. He would not find his car for another hour and a half.

During the course of his life, he had wasted countless hours searching for his car in shopping-center parking lots and on city streets. At home and at work, he would go through a similar daily ritual of looking for his keys, his coat, his wallet, or an important file that he needed. At first, his associates found this little routine amusing and would tease him about it. Later, they began to wonder about the bizarre behavior.

The man not only lost things, but he also had a terrible sense of direction. When walking or driving in an unfamiliar area, he would quickly become disoriented. Leaving a movie theater and finding his car was like throwing dice. Occasionally he might be lucky and select the right exit. More likely than not he would end up on the wrong side of the theater.

The man even became lost in familiar territory. He could never figure out if he was heading toward or away from his destination, nor could he recall if he had been on a particular road before, unless he had driven there at least three times previously. He marveled at people who could figure out the direction in which they were driving on the freeway.

Because his father had also had a poor sense of direction and his mother would become hopelessly lost when driving, the man had concluded that his inadequate homing instinct was a bad genetic joke. Resigned to being in a state of continual disorientation, he had learned to compensate by allowing extra time to look for his keys or find his way.

One day the man discussed his problem with a friend who listened sympathetically and then suggested a simple solution. "Each time you park your car, pretend that your eyes are a camera. Look around you and sight your 'lens' on a particular object. This object might be the airport control tower or the sign on a department store. Imagine yourself actually taking a picture of the object and hearing the shutter click. By consciously focusing your mind on the landmark, you will imprint the geographical data, and you should be able to find your way back to your car."

The system worked magnificently. At first, the man would occasionally forget to use his "camera" and would become disoriented. When he did use the system, however, he had no difficulty finding his car or his keys. Although his navigational confidence was still tenuous, he felt less vulnerable and stupid and would become lost only when he allowed himself to become oblivious to his surroundings. The camera even worked on the highway. As he drove toward his destination, he trained himself to take a mental picture of landmarks. On the return trip, he would search for the landmarks to assure himself that he was heading in the right direction. He still had an intrinsically poor sense of direction, but he spent considerably less time looking for his car, the keys, or the right direction on the freeway.

BARRIERS TO SMART THINKING

As you read the previous anecdote, you may have wondered how a person of normal intelligence could be so dense. Remembering where you park your car or where you leave your keys certainly does not require a great deal of brilliance. It does, however, require that the person who has a poor natural homing instinct be able to devise an effective strategy for dealing with his deficiency.

Perceiving solutions to another person's problems is, of course, far easier than finding solutions to one's own problems. The sage advice of Dear Abby and Ann Landers testifies to the fact that insight and wisdom are directly proportional to one's distance from the drama. (By the way, be careful not to chuckle too loudly at our disoriented friend. You are laughing at *me!*)

The person struggling with a significant or recurring problem rarely has the luxury of perspective and distance. Being on the "front lines" creates a greater sense of urgency and offers a different view. Nevertheless, it is the capacity to achieve perspective that permits adults—and children—to solve problems. Developing this capacity is a cornerstone of smart thinking.

UNSTRAPPING THE PROTECTIVE ARMOR

Every human being has deficiencies. For a child, these deficits may involve remembering how to spell or how to master the multiplication tables. For an adult, the deficiencies may take the form of chronic forgetfulness, disorientation or disorganization.

A child who feels vulnerable typically spends a great deal of emotional and physical energy protecting himself from his real or imagined weaknesses. The child's defense mechanisms often become an integral part of his identity and his personality.

Even the very talented child may be acutely aware of—and sensitive to—his limitations. A very bright 13-year-old, for example, may be having difficulty with Spanish. By the end of the school year, she is certain that she will never be able to learn to master a foreign language. Nevertheless, she somehow makes it through the foreign language requirements in high school and in college and ultimately becomes a highly accomplished scientist. Despite her many accomplishments, she remains convinced that she is hopelessly inept in the area of foreign languages.

The origins of a child's protective behavior can usually be traced to early childhood. Negative experiences during these formative years almost invariably imprint correspondingly negative associations on a child's unconscious mind. This imprinting process may begin in kindergarten or even earlier.

Imagine a 5-year-old who has difficulty with fine-motor tasks and whose drawings appear disjointed and distorted. If other children (or even the child's parents) tease her about her artwork, the child may conclude that she is incompetent. To protect herself, she may begin to avoid anything having to do with art. Before long, she becomes resigned to her "inadequacy" and develops an aversion to anything that requires creativity or rudimentary artistic ability. As an adult, she decides that because of her incompetence, she must rely on interior decorators to furnish her home and upon salespeople to tell her what clothes to buy.

Although a child's deficiency may be quite insignificant (or even imagined), the deficiency may appear monumental to the child. If unresolved, the deficit could become so magnified and distorted in the child's mind that it assumes the dimensions of a seemingly insurmountable barrier. Ironically, the kindergartner who acquired profoundly negative associations with art actually might have had potential artistic talent that could have been developed with proper instruction and encouragement.

"I AIN'T GOOD AT THAT!"

Aptitude must be included in the equation that produces smart thinking. As a specialized form of intelligence, aptitude usually manifests itself in a specific skill or ability.

Most human beings have aptitude in one or more areas. For some, the facility may be in the area of mechanics. For others, it may be in the area of art or athletics.

A child's specific aptitudes equip him to do certain tasks with ease, while his specific aptitude deficits make other tasks more difficult. If the child's imprinted associations with one of his deficit areas are profoundly negative, he may conclude that he is incapable of solving any problem requiring those skills in which he feels deficient. *Once a child becomes convinced that a task is impossible, the task becomes impossible.* Negative expectations are usually self-fulfilling.

Because of frustrating experiences as a child, a renowned and talented opera singer may conclude that she is mechanically inept. Perhaps she tried to assemble something and went to her father for assistance. Without consciously intending to "put her down," he teased her about her clumsiness. For the first time, she became acutely aware of a deficiency, and she was embarrassed because she sensed that she had disappointed her father. The seeds for an "I can't do that" attitude were planted, and each time the child attempted something mechanical and experienced frustration, the seeds were fertilized. Over the years, the roots of the girl's negative associations with mechanics begin to spread and take hold. By the time she becomes an adult, the prospect of hooking up a new stereo system completely intimidates her, and she asks a friend to do it for her. Convinced that she is incompetent, she protects herself by avoiding any task that might require mechanical problem-solving skills.

In theory, any person of average intelligence could learn how to hook up a stereo system. With proper instruction and practice, the opera singer probably could have become relatively adept at performing basic mechanical tasks. This assumes, of course, that she subsequently had sufficient positive experiences to offset the aversion to mechanical operations im-

35

printed during her early childhood. If, however, she cannot reorient her negative mind-set and negative expectations, she may become permanently convinced that she is hopelessly inept.

ORCHESTRATING SUCCESS

Parents who are concerned that their child has a negative mind-set about her own abilities can significantly reduce the risk of the child developing an "I ain't good at that" attitude by applying the following guidelines:

★ *Show your child how to capitalize upon her natural ability and intelligence* (e.g., encourage her to develop her natural artistic or athletic ability).

★ *Intentionally create opportunities for your child to experience success* (e.g., propose projects at which your child is certain to do well— and help if appropriate).

★ *Help your child discover that she is capable and competent* (e.g., emphasize that many children or adults could not do what she has done).

Once convinced that she has the ability to achieve, your child can begin to define what she wants out of life and identify the obstacles standing in her way. As she learns to use her natural resources, she will discover all sorts of ingenious ways to overcome or compensate for any deficits she might have. This is the essence of smart thinking.

Providing guidance and showing your child how to identify, analyze, overcome, or bypass life's inevitable roadblocks does not mean taking ownership of your child's problem. For example, let's assume your daughter has poor visual memory skills (difficulty visualizing and remembering the letters in words). As a consequence, she is a poor speller. To overcome the problem, she must either improve her visual memory skills or find another way to master the material. She may need to develop several different techniques for remembering how non-phonetic words are spelled. For example, she might close her eyes and see the word "receive" imprinted on the back of her eyelids. If she is a kinesthetic learner (one who learns by feel and touch), she might use the tiles from a Scrabble game to reinforce how the words are put together. She might also trace the letters repeatedly with her finger on a piece of sandpaper or carve them into a big cookie tray filled with a layer of plastic clay.

The smart child trains himself to evaluate each situation to determine whether it is smart to crash through a road block or smarter to go around it.

For example, a talented college football player being pursued by several professional teams may conclude that he lacks the expertise to make important business and career decisions. Upon the recommendation of his parents, he decides to hire a first-rate agent and a business manager. Realizing that getting help is smart and strategic, he employs experts to guide him in areas in which he lacks experience. He is thus able to focus his energy and talents on the area where he does have expertise—sports.

Structuring success is especially critical when parents perceive that their child is beginning to manifest avoidance behavior. Had the parents of the opera singer been perceptive, they could have undoubtedly intervened and helped her overcome her phobic reaction to mechanical operations. If negative associations and psychological scarring are to be avoided, it is critical that you identify indications of phobic behavior in your child as early as possible. (*Note:* To help you do this, you will find attitude checklists for you and your child to complete later in this chapter).

HITCHING UP THE HORSES

Intelligence, aptitude, and smartness are the primary sources of a child's capacity to solve life's problems. When properly matched and harnessed, this team of intellectual "horses" has the capacity to generate tremendous power.

Sometimes a child has only one horse pulling his sled. One youngster may be highly intelligent and competent in math, but may lack specific aptitude in language arts. A second child may have highly developed aptitude in graphic design but may test in the average range on an IQ test. Despite his intellectual limitations, the child's specific aptitude equips him to become very successful in his chosen field.

Some children are missing a lead horse in their intellectual team. As a consequence, their efforts are poorly coordinated. The classic example of this phenomenon is the child who possesses superior general intelligence and aptitude in specific areas, but who does not act smart. Because he lacks planning, organizational and strategic-thinking skills, his intellectual and emotional energies remain unfocused. As a result, he muddles through school and through life, wasting a great deal of natural talent.

There is another category of children. Although these children may be pulled by only one horse, the horse is clever and sure-footed. He can usually figure out how to avoid the steep, treacherous hills or, when necessary, how to get over them quickly and safely. "Street-smart" children fall into this category. They may not have an especially high IQ nor any remarkable specific aptitude, but they are able to do what is necessary to prevail. Typically described as "survivors," these children have an uncanny ability to land on their feet when they jump or when they stumble.

The smart child uses the resources that are available. He is observant and responsive to life's lessons, and he learns from his experiences. He quickly realizes that it is not clever to tweak the nose of the toughest kid in the class.

Every child can be taught how to create a more balanced and powerful propulsion system. When faced with a challenge, he can supercharge this propulsion system by asking himself key problem-solving questions such as: "I made this mistake before. How can I avoid making it again? What am I trying to achieve, and how can I best achieve it?"

When intelligence, aptitude, and smartness are pulling in the same direction, they can convert a sled into the equivalent of a four-wheel-drive jeep. Conversely, when mismatched or poorly harnessed, they will pull inefficiently and cause the sled to lurch and slide from side to side. Unfortunately, the world is full of lurching sleds that cannot make it up the hill.

It is important to note that any child, even one who acts smart under most conditions, can occasionally become sidetracked because of emotional or environmental factors. For example, a conscientious high school student who normally does first-rate work may become uncharacteristically distracted by social events and a new boyfriend. She begins to coast in school and puts off her English essay until the last day. As she struggles to complete her assignment at 11 p.m., she is sleepy and inattentive. Lacking the time and energy to revise and proofread her work, she submits a report of marginal quality. Although bright, talented, and usually quite strategic, she suffers the consequences of her lack of planning. Her grade on the essay is a C-.

When a child becomes seriously sidetracked, some form of parental intervention is required. The starting point in the process of providing guidance and feedback is a frank, non-demeaning discussion of the issues (dialogues demonstrating this type of communication are found later in this chapter). This examination process may be sufficient, and the teenager may voluntarily eliminate his counterproductive behavior. If not, more stringent guidelines and performance standards may be required. Should the behavior persist, the teenager should be monitored closely, and his parents may need to consult a mental-health professional.[1]

---

[1]For a more complete explanation of this issue, see *Kids Who Underachieve*, (Lawrence J. Greene), Simon & Schuster, New York, 1985.

38

ATTITUDES THAT DEFEAT SMARTNESS

A powerful instinct compels human beings to protect themselves from their weaknesses, vulnerabilities and insecurities. In modern society, this instinct manifests itself primarily in the form of psychological or emotional defense mechanisms. These mechanisms usually undermine a child's capacity to function productively.

The child perceiving an intellectual or physical limitation has five basic response options:

1. He can deny that he has a limitation.
2. He can accept his limitation and resign himself.
3. He can avoid confronting situations in which he feels vulnerable.
4. He can compensate for the limitation by developing alternative means for attaining his objectives.
5. He can develop other talents that permit him to excel.

The protective instinct may run rampant in the case of some children. To insulate themselves from frustration and failure, insecure children may begin to develop increasingly distorted perceptions and behaviors. As these distortions become enmeshed in their self-concepts, they frequently create formidable barriers to achievement.

A child's perceptions about his abilities inevitably influence the goals that he sets for himself. The child who concludes in elementary school that he is "dumb" in math may also conclude that he is dumb in other areas of his life. Although his perceptions about his abilities may be inaccurate, they constitute the child's reality. Each incorrect math problem and each poor grade on a quiz or a test will reinforce his negative feelings about his abilities. Without intervention, the child's conviction that he is incompetent will undermine his already tenuous self-esteem and self-confidence. Although he may develop competencies in other areas, it is more likely that he will simply lower his level of expectations. Once he does, his fate is sealed.

Smart children, of course, also have deficiencies. In most instances, however, they figure out how to overcome or compensate successfully for these deficiencies. This does not mean that the smart child never needs help. He can become stymied by a problem that he may not be able to resolve on his own. The talented baseball player, for example, who is in a batting slump could undoubtedly benefit from some expert coaching.

The child who does not intuitively think smart has a special need for guidance and instruction. Such a child must be helped to examine the

39

attitudes and behaviors that are blocking his achievement and interfering with the development of effective problem-solving skills.

BARRIERS TO ACHIEVEMENT

Depending on the circumstances, a child's choice to compensate for a deficiency or to avoid a problem may indicate smart thinking or not-so-smart thinking. A student who struggles through freshman math in high school may decide that once he fulfills his college math requirement, he will never take another math course. His aversion to math may persist into adulthood, and he may relegate the responsibilities for paying the bills, reconciling the family checkbook, and gathering the data for the tax return to his wife. Although his compensatory system is pragmatic, the avoidance mechanism places him in a very vulnerable position, especially if his wife becomes unable to perform her assigned function. The man's vulnerability and his awareness of his math inadequacies cannot help but have a negative effect on his self-esteem and self-concept. In the final analysis, his compensatory system offers little protection and security.

Thwarted children usually evolve into thwarted adults. Despite their attempts to camouflage their deficiencies by making excuses, rationalizing, or even making fun of themselves, phobic adults are profoundly affected by their real or imagined inadequacies. Although the previously described opera singer may joke with her friends about her mechanical incompetence, she will probably not be laughing when the circuit breaker shuts down at 9 p.m. as she is preparing for an audition the following morning. Convinced that she is incapable of figuring out which switch to flip through trial and error, she permits herself to be controlled by the "I can't do this. I'm too stupid." tape that was recorded when she was a child. This same response might occur when she tries to attach the wiper blade on her car during a rain storm. Re-experiencing familiar feelings of incompetence, her stress triggers an anxiety chain reaction, and she reverts to feeling like a mechanically inept 8-year-old.

MANIPULATIVE BEHAVIOR

By the age of eight, most children have already acquired a vast storehouse of information and experience about life. They have been conditioned to avoid life-threatening situations such as running into the street, playing with matches, and talking to strangers. They have also developed a keen intuition about people and can usually sense which ones to trust and which ones to avoid.

By the age of eight, most children have also acquired a spectrum of psychological survival skills. They have learned how to regulate certain aspects of their environment and learned how to control the responses they elicit from friends and adults. This control may be positive or negative. Patterns of negative control include such behaviors as manipulation, resistance, denial or rationalization. For example, a child who is clearly struggling in school may attempt to deny that he has a problem by blaming the teacher or by arguing that the teacher is boring. Not all control, however, is negative. The child who decides to train hard in gymnastics may be motivated by a desire to impress her coach and her parents with her skills and effort. If her performance pleases her coach, improves her chances of making the team, and makes her feel good, the behavior would have to be considered productive and smart.

Some children feel compelled to exert absolute control over their environment and the people with whom they interact. For example, a child may throw temper tantrums, and as a result, get what he wants. The association the child is imprinting with the payoff for his behavior could influence his entire life. By being able to elicit this type of response, the child learns that the squeaky wheel gets the oil. If he concludes that squeaking is the only way to get what he wants, he will probably become either highly obnoxious or highly manipulative.

A child is driven to control people and situations for complex reasons. Usually, the underlying source of the behavior is fear, insecurity and low self-esteem. Secure, confident children don't need to run every show.

Manipulative behavior can assume many different forms. One child may discover that if she mopes and complains, her parents will appease her and give in. Another may discover that if he feigns helplessness, his parents will invariably rescue him.

As previously stated, all forms of control need not be manipulative, devious or dishonest. For instance, a child may discover the positive value of giving people compliments. If the compliments are insincere, they are manipulative. If the compliments are genuine and represent a sincere effort to acknowledge others, they would not be manipulative, even if the habit of giving compliments works to the child's advantage. It should also be noted that some children (and adults) give compliments primarily because they want to be liked. Such behavior clearly has manipulative undertones.

The ability to regulate certain situations can be vital to emotional, physical or financial survival. For example, a person must be able to negotiate effectively with a salesman at an automobile dealership. By exerting control during the negotiation process, she reduces her vulnerability to sales ploys and pressure. She will also need to learn when it is most opportune to approach her boss about a raise. The function and intent of the behavior must be considered in order to determine whether or not the behavior is honest, appropriate and smart.

Before parents can deal effectively with manipulative behavior, they must first be able to detect it. To do so, they must train themselves to listen to their child on multiple levels. This requires distinguishing the facts (a poor grade on a math test) from interpretations, conclusions, opinions, and feelings ("My teacher wasn't being fair!").

Once parents are able to classify the content of the communication, they can respond to facts with problem-solving strategies ("Perhaps we need to get you a tutor.") and to interpretations, conclusions, opinions and feelings with empathy ("You seem very upset about your grades"). Parents who develop their capacity to listen on multiple levels and classify what they are hearing usually discover that they can respond more effectively to manipulative, counterproductive behavior.

Parents who suspect that their child is manipulative must first decide if their child's attempt to control specific events is reasonable or devious. Temper tantrums, lies, half-truths, and guile clearly fall into the category of devious control. Children using such techniques, however, may not be consciously aware of what they are doing. This is especially true when manipulative behavior has become a habit. Changing these patterns can test the patience and forbearance of even the most dedicated parents.

Most parents recognize their responsibility to discourage counterproductive, manipulative behavior. Responding appropriately to this conduct and resisting the natural temptation to become angry can be a challenge. If positive behavioral changes are to occur, resistance and resentment must be defused. Although it is possible to force a child to change his behavior, it is usually easier and far more effective to elicit the child's cooperation and active participation in the process. The tone and mood that parents establish during discussions of behavioral issues are of vital importance. Parents who are derogatory or confrontive should expect either overt or covert resistance. Frontal assaults cannot help but trigger defensiveness. Parents who use a gentler approach ("Is it possible that . . .?" or "How might someone describe your behavior?") usually encounter far less resistance.

Selecting a calm moment is essential if you are planning to broach the issue of manipulative behavior with your child. The first step is to identify the specific behavior that concerns you. The next step is to explain why you find this trait objectionable.

You must recognize, however, that a discussion rarely succeeds in changing entrenched behavior patterns, especially when a child has become accustomed to testing the rules and the limits. If the behavior recurs, you might respond, "I feel that you are trying to manipulate me, and I will not accept this behavior. Tell me what actually happened." If the child's manipulation takes the form of a predictable temper tantrum or door-slamming, you might respond, "I can see you're angry. You may go to your room and be as angry as you wish. When you are ready to talk calmly about how you're feeling, come out and we will talk." Parents perceiving chronic patterns of anger or self-destructive behavior should consult with a mental-health professional.

DETERMINING IF YOUR CHILD HAS A NEGATIVE MIND-SET

The following checklist is designed to help you identify the negative attitudes that can defeat smart thinking and undermine your child's ability to resolve problems. Later in the chapter you will find a second checklist for your child to complete. This second checklist has two functions: to stimulate parent-child communication and to introduce activities designed to encourage the positive attitudes that lead to smart thinking.

Checklist for Parent *ATTITUDES*

Code: 0 = Never   1 = Rarely
      2 = Sometimes   3 = Often   4 = Always

My child is willing to take reasonable risks.   _____

My child is enthusiastic about seeking and   _____
accepting new challenges.

My child enjoys finding solutions to problems.   _____

My child likes to test and stretch his or her   _____
limits.

My child has faith in his or her ability to   _____
succeed at whatever he or she undertakes.

My child completes projects.   _____

My child takes pride in doing a first-rate job.   _____

My child perseveres despite setbacks.   _____

My child feels he or she deserves to "win." _____

My child feels he or she is a valuable person. _____

My child feels he or she is intelligent. _____

Interpreting the Checklist

A pattern of 0's, 1's and 2's suggests that your child's attitudes about his abilities are undermining smart thinking and achievement-oriented performance. A total score below 25 suggests attitudes that could sabotage smart thinking.

Counterproductive attitudes reflect a child's unconscious need to protect himself from feeling inadequate. Traits such as giving up when things get difficult or leaving projects incomplete are clearly avoidance mechanisms. The behaviors suggest that your child has had painful experiences in school, at home, or with friends and that these experiences have damaged him. In the following sections of this chapter, you will find specific methods for reorienting self-defeating attitudes.

PROVIDING YOUR CHILD WITH PROBLEM-SOLVING RESOURCES

Smart children recognize that they have several options for handling problems. Such children usually perceive problems as challenges that they can confront and surmount. Before they can win these battles, however, they must properly "arm" themselves.

Children with a high Smartness Quotient discover, on their own, that there are ways to prepare for confronting challenges. Other children need to be taught the basic steps that will permit them to prevail.

As a parent, you play a pivotal role in training your child to deal successfully with challenges. When confronted with a problem, your child must learn how to apply the basic steps that facilitate problem-solving.

1. Define the challenge or problem.
2. Create a strategy that neutralizes deficiencies and allows me to prevail over the challenge. (e.g., "How might someone else deal with this? I will think of somebody who can handle this type of problem. How might he/she approach it?")
3. Find alternative means for getting from point A to point B should I become stuck or blocked.

By guiding your child through a process of solution-oriented problem analysis, you can help him internalize the steps. Developing competency with the method is like learning to type. Practice and effort are essential. With sufficient practice, your child should be able to integrate the method into his response patterns so that it becomes a reflex. The ultimate objective is for your child to have the presence of mind to stop, think analytically, and then act smart when he is faced with a challenging situation.

It is important that you impress upon your child that he already possesses the resources to solve many of the problems he faces. He simply needs to learn how to tap into these resources. Children generally relate well to analogies. For example, you might describe how a person with a physical handicap might use her ingenuity to compensate for a physical limitation. By examining the hypothetical person's problem-solving process with your child, you are helping him appreciate the value of systematic, strategic thinking.

Below you will find a dialogue that models how you could present the steps to your child. The dialogue leads the child through the problem-solving method and shows how it can be used to neutralize the problem. The child in the dialogue is 10 years old. The language can be simplified for younger children or "upgraded" for teenagers.

MODEL DIALOGUE #3
PROBLEM-SOLVING TECHNIQUES
Children ages 7-12

Parent: You've told me that you are upset because your soccer coach is not letting you play as much as you would like. Is this true?

Child: Yes.

Parent: You've seen several people in wheelchairs, haven't you?

Child: Yeah.

Parent: Do you think that a person in a wheelchair would have a difficult time getting something down from a kitchen shelf if she were unable to get out of the chair?

Child: Yeah.

Parent: What could she do to solve her problem?

Child: She could get someone else to do it for her.

Parent: But what would happen if no one else was home and the woman needed a glass for water?

Child: I don't know.

Parent: Could you think of a way to solve the problem?

Child: She could get a carpenter to build lower shelves.

Parent: That's a super idea! But what if she doesn't have enough money to hire a carpenter or buy lumber. Are there any other possible solutions?

Child: Maybe she could make something to help her get things down from the shelf.

Parent: Another super idea! Let's see if we could figure out what she could do. Any ideas?

Child: A stick with a hook on the end.

Parent: Yeah! Or maybe she could in some way attach a flat, thin piece of metal to the end of a broom handle. Let's see if we can draw something that would work.

Parent: What would have happened if the woman couldn't design something to get things down from the shelves in her kitchen?

Child: She would be sad.

Parent: And frustrated.

Child: Yeah. When she needs a bowl or something, she wouldn't be able to get it.

Parent: You're right. What do you think about people giving up when they have a difficult problem?

Child: They shouldn't give up.

Parent: Let's say you ran into a problem that seemed enormous. Would you give up?

Child: No.

Parent: Let's say you were striking out a lot when you played baseball. What could you do?

Child: I could talk to the coach.

Parent: Yes.

Child: He could tell me what I was doing wrong.

46

Parent: You might be taking your eye off the ball. Anything else you could do?

Child: I could practice—at a batting cage.

Parent: That's right. So you see, the first step is to admit you have a problem. The next step is to think about what you need to do in order to solve the problem. If the woman in the wheelchair couldn't figure out how to solve her problem, she might have asked you. You would have helped her find a solution! You, too, may someday have to ask someone else for help, especially if you can't figure out how to solve a problem yourself. That's why discussing a problem with someone else can help you find a solution. Two people can put their heads together and figure out a solution. It's called brainstorming, and this technique cannot only be useful, it can be a lot of fun. Let's see if we can use it to solve your problem with your soccer coach. First of all, what is the problem?

Child: The coach won't let me play as much as I want.

Parent: Do you feel that the coach thinks you're a good player?

Child: I think so. I scored two goals already this year.

Parent: What about practice. Are you getting there on time and hustling?

Child: Well, not really.

Parent: Tell me what's happening.

Child: He gets mad at me for fooling around. He says I'm not paying attention to what I am doing. I get bored if the ball is on the other side of the field.

Parent: I suppose that could turn the coach off.

Child: Yeah.

Parent: You are a good soccer player, and you've proved it by scoring two goals. If you want to play more, what do you think you have to do?

Child: Play harder.

Parent: Yeah. And maybe do what during practice?

Child: Concentrate on what's going on.

Parent:	I wonder how you could impress the coach with the changes you are going to make.
Child:	I could tell him.
Parent:	That might work. What else could you do?
Child:	I could show him.
Parent:	I agree. Guess what? We've just brainstormed a solution to your problem!

The first step in demonstrating how to solve problems is to establish a context that encourages problem-solving. The parent in the preceding dialogue intentionally creates such a context. Several key elements can be identified:

1. The parent chooses an analogy that is non-threatening and an analogy to which the child can relate.
2. The parent draws a parallel that stimulates the child to think analytically.
3. The parent exposes the child to a creative, problem-solving process.
4. The parent urges the child to offer suggestions.
5. The parent is careful to acknowledge the child's suggestions.
6. The parent establishes trust.
7. The parent models a workable system.
8. The parent encourages a work-together attitude.
9. The parent helps the child realize that a problem that might seem unsolvable is actually solvable.

You will note that the parent resists the temptation to take ownership of the child's problem. He doesn't say, "Well, that seems unfair, especially if you are a good player. I'm going to speak to the coach about this!" Had the parent done so, he would have denied the child an opportunity to solve his own problem.

The parent also resists the temptation to lecture or to make excuses for the coach. He doesn't say, "Well, Son, the coach has to give all the children a chance to play." (This response would have immediately been classified by the child as "parent talk.") Nor does the parent say, "If you would stop goofing off in practice, maybe you would get more playing time."

You can play a vital role in helping your child learn how to examine key events in his or her life. This process of encouraging your child to "digest" life's lessons is central to developing smart-thinking skills. By urging your child to think about what is happening, you make it possible for him to relinquish the counterproductive behaviors and negative thoughts that undermine success and achievement.

DEVELOPING YOUR CHILD'S SMARTNESS QUOTIENT

With parental guidance virtually every child can become smarter. Unlike IQ, which is genetically based, a child's Smartness Quotient (SQ) can be developed and nurtured.

A powerful system for improving a child's problem-solving ability and for increasing his SQ can be represented by the acronym DIBS.

D(define) the problem. (For example: "I get nervous when I take a test, and as a result, I do poorly.")

I(investigate) the triggers that cause the problem and investigate the related issues. (For example: "I get anxious about not being able to remember the information that I have studied. I know that you and Dad want me to do well, and I feel that if I do poorly, you will be disappointed in me.")

B(brainstorm) ideas about how to deal with the problem. (For example: "I could learn how to relax before taking a test.")

S(select) an idea from the brainstorming to try. (For example: "Before my next biology test, I'll close my eyes and breathe deeply two or three times. I'll spend 30 seconds consciously trying to relax before beginning to answer the questions on the test.")

The _DIBS System_ trains your child to look for the underlying issues when he is confronted with a problem. The child who develops the habit of examining these issues has acquired a powerful resource.

The objective of the DIBS System is the same as that of the dialogue method: to help your child achieve insight. The DIBS System offers an alternative approach with which you might feel more comfortable. In this and subsequent chapters, your child will be given many opportunities to practice and master the system.

As your child achieves insight into his experiences, problems and responses, he will be gaining insight into himself. This insight is one of the cornerstones of smart thinking. (The subject of introspection will be examined in depth in Chapter 3.)

Because the DIBS System encourages self-assessment, it is advisable to have your child complete the following attitude inventory before proceeding.

ENCOURAGING YOUR CHILD TO ASSESS HIS OR HER ATTITUDES

Before asking your child to complete the following attitude checklist, carefully consider how you might best present it. (You will note that this inventory is similar to the one you completed earlier in the chapter.) It is important that you present the inventory in a non-threatening way. You might say, "We have already done some activities involving cause and effect. Before doing other activities with you, I'd like you to fill out the following checklist. Later, when we have completed the book, I am going to ask you to fill out another inventory, and we can compare the results."

The inventory can be used with children from ages 7 to 17. You will find that certain questions are obviously more applicable to older children, and you should use your discretion and eliminate questions that you feel are non-relevant for your child. Younger children will probably need some assistance and perhaps an explanation of some of the statements.

Some children may prefer to complete the survey without your assistance. Others may want help. If you do help your child, do not provide the "answers." Let your child provide his or her own responses to the statements. If your child is unsure about how to respond to a particular statement, suggest that he or she mark the first thing that comes to mind. If your child is confused about what a word means (for example, the word "setbacks"), attempt to explain it in language your child can understand.

Do not use your child's responses as a justification for a lecture or a sermon about the importance of a "good" attitude! The purpose of the inventory is to initiate communication and to create a context for the brainstorming and problem-solving activities that follow.

Checklist for Child
ATTITUDES

Code: 0 = Never 1 = Rarely
      2 = Sometimes 3 = Often 4 = Always

I like challenges.   _____

It's important that I do well in school.   _____

I enjoy finding and correcting my mistakes.   _____

I believe that I can do a good job if I want to.   _____

I can do good work even if I am not very   _____
excited about the project.

50

I like to test myself to find out how good I am.   _____

I can handle setbacks.   _____

I learn from mistakes and try not to make the same   _____
mistakes again.

I am willing to accept help when I am stuck or   _____
confused.

I believe that my friends respect me.   _____

I believe that my teachers respect me.   _____

I believe that my parents respect me.   _____

People think that I am a hard worker.   _____

I like school.   _____

I think I am smart.   _____

I finish projects that I start.   _____

I enjoy getting good grades.   _____

I enjoy developing my skills and talents.   _____

I enjoy finding solutions to problems.   _____

I am not afraid to take a risk and try something   _____
difficult.

TOTAL   _____

Interpreting the Checklist

You may want to discuss the statements and responses with your child
after he or she completes them. You might explain that a pattern of 0's, 1's,
and 2's suggests that some work needs to be done in the area of developing
a more positive attitude. Emphasize that the score is totaled so that you and
your child can compare the results with a second checklist that will be
filled out after having completed the activities in the book.

Although an examination of your child's specific responses to the statements on the checklist might be beneficial at this time, it is not essential
that there be discussion. This is true even if there is a pattern of 0's, 1's and
2's. Do not force your child to analyze or elaborate upon the responses if
you sense resistance. The two primary goals of the attitude checklist are to
provide a baseline and to encourage your child to begin thinking about his

51

or her attitudes. Subsequent activities will offer an opportunity for further exploration.

WORKING SUCCESSFULLY WITH YOUR CHILD

Your child's problem-solving skills and facility with the DIBS System will improve with practice. The following scenarios and problems are intended to provide an opportunity for practice.

The first set of activities is directed toward children in the second through seventh grades. The second set is directed toward teenagers. As you examine the material, other perhaps more relevant subjects besides the ones described in this book may occur either to you or your child. Do not hesitate to substitute these subjects for the scenarios described below. Also, do not feel that you have to cover all of the issues raised below.

The D(define) I(investigate) B(brainstorm) S(select) System is sequential. By showing your child how to explore the underlying issues systematically, you are achieving three important objectives:

1. You are providing your child with an opportunity to practice creative problem-solving.
2. You are encouraging your child to develop his ingenuity.
3. You are showing your child how to increase his Smartness Quotient.

Additional issues related to the topics you and your child are discussing can be introduced either as questions or statements (e.g., "I wonder how . .."). It is important to resist the temptation to bombard your child with questions. Sometimes using the third person as opposed to the second person can be less threatening for a child who is reluctant to discuss feelings. For example, you might ask, "If your friend were upset because her little sister was coming into her room and borrowing things, what could she do?"

Be prepared to listen actively, supportively and non-judgmentally, and by all means avoid giving your child "the third degree." You might simply respond to your child's statements by saying, "That's interesting." You might then say, "Have you ever considered . . .?" The purpose of these exercises is to encourage brainstorming and to help your child integrate the DIBS System into his response to problems and challenges. Although you can and should provide guidance, resist the temptation to solve the problems. By giving the answers, you defeat the intent of the system, which is to develop *your child's* thinking skills.

It is quite common for a child to respond to a question or a statement with "I don't know." Use your judgment. It may be advisable to probe more deeply, or it may be advisable to let the matter drop. You might say, "Think about it, and we'll talk about it later." Children, like adults, are often quite resistant to examining their feelings, especially if these feelings are associated with pain or anger.

Please note that there are no "correct" solutions to the problems described. Your child may suggest solutions that are unique and distinctive. This should be encouraged, as long as the solutions are reasonable. If they are not, the inconsistencies in logic can be pointed out and discussed without demeaning or criticizing your child. Techniques for doing this are modeled later in the chapter. Remember, your objective is not to find fault but to encourage your child to think analytically, strategically and creatively.

The DIBS System
Children ages 7-12

Define Problem:	Let's imagine that my boss wants to transfer me to an office in another state.
Investigate Issues:	Is it fair for her to ask me to move?
	Would it be fair for me to ask my family to go to another part of the country?
	What could happen if I refused to accept the transfer?
	What are the benefits for me if I accept the transfer?
	How would moving affect your mother?
	How would moving affect you?
	I wonder what adjustments you would have to make.
	Could you make those adjustments? How would you feel?
	How do you think Mom would feel? How do you think I would feel?
Brainstorm:	Let's make a list of reasons why I should turn down the transfer.

Let's make a list of reasons why I should accept the transfer.

Let's think of some things that I could tell my boss if I wanted to try to convince her to let me stay here.

Select: "Tomorrow I'm going to meet with my boss and present her with my reasons for wanting/not wanting the transfer."

★ ★ ★ ★

Define Problem: Let's assume your little sister is coming into your room and borrowing things that belong to you.

Investigate Issues: How do you feel about what is happening?

Do you think your sister understands how her behavior is making you feel?

I wonder why your sister might want things that belong to you. Any ideas?

If you had an older sister, might you want to borrow her things?

Do you sometimes borrow things that belong to your mom or your friends?

Have you done anything to correct the problem?

I wonder why these measures haven't been as successful as you would have liked. Any ideas?

Can you think of any measures you haven't tried yet that could possibly solve the problem?

How could you present the problem to your sister in terms she could understand?

Tell me what you could do if she continues to borrow things without your permission, or if she fails to return them.

Brainstorm: Let's make a list of things you might do to solve this problem.

Select: You could speak to your sister tonight about why you don't want her to borrow your things without

54

your permission. You might give her a list of things she can borrow and a list of things she can't borrow.

★ ★ ★ ★

Define Problem: The child sitting next to you is getting in trouble for talking in class and disturbing other children. (Using the third person may trigger less defensiveness and/or resistance.)

Investigate Issues: Could you tell me what you think the teacher is upset about?

Do you feel that the teacher should be upset with the child?

Could the child change her behavior so that she would no longer get into trouble?

Brainstorm: Let's see what she might do to solve the problem.

Would it help for the child and her parents to have a conference with the teacher?

Could the child ask the teacher to move her desk?

Could she and her parents make up a list of behaviors she wants to change, and could she then ask the teacher to fill out a behavior report card each day?

(Ideally, your child will be coming up with ideas of his or her own. Encourage this! Do not feel you have to use the ideas presented here. The important thing is to elicit ideas from your child.)

Select: The child could design the behavior report card so that the teacher could put a check after each behavior when she does well in that area on that day.

★ ★ ★ ★

Define Problem: You feel that we are always bugging you about keeping your room clean.

Investigate Issues: Should parents complain to their children about their rooms being messy or dirty?

55

Who "owns" a child's room, the child or her parents?

Should kids be required to keep their rooms neat?

Do parents have "rights?" (Explain the term if necessary.)

Could you tell me what you feel "kids rights" are?

Can parents and kids make compromises? (Explain this concept, if necessary, by giving an example of a compromise.)

I wonder how we could arrive at a compromise to restore peace in the family.

What should the consequences be if someone doesn't live up to his side of the bargain?

Brainstorm: Let's see how this problem could be solved. Let's start by agreeing on a reasonable list of kids' rights and a list of parents' rights.

Select: The child could work on improving one behavior each week. For instance, she could agree to hang up her clothes. The next week she might work on making her bed each morning. She would, of course, continue to hang up her clothes.

The DIBS System
Teenagers ages 13-17

Define Problem: I'm curious about how you might respond to this problem. Let's say I am having an argument with my business partner. I feel that he is coming into work late and taking extra holidays. He feels that he is doing his fair share of the work.

Investigate Issues: Do I have a right to keep track of my partner's hours?

How should I respond if he feels he can get the job done in fewer hours than I think is reasonable, and I disagree with his assessment?

Can partners be equal partners if they work unequal hours?

I wonder how I might best express my displeasure?

How should someone respond if the other person becomes defensive?

How can we decide how much work is required to do the job well?

Brainstorm: My partner and I could make up a list of priorities, tasks, and responsibilities, and decide about the time required to perform them. We could then decide who will be responsible for the tasks. Periodic evaluation meetings could be held to see how things are going. [Continue brainstorming.]

Select: We could set up a meeting on Monday, and we could discuss what each of our responsibilities is. Once we agree, we could make up a list and periodically review the situation to make sure that we are each doing what we agreed to do.

★ ★ ★ ★

Define Problem: You are upset because we have imposed a curfew on you.

**Investigate
Issues:** Do you think parents have the right to impose rules on teenagers?

Do you feel we as parents should have a reason for each one of our rules?

I wonder why rules and laws are created.

Could you tell me why you think we have established a curfew?

What do you feel is unreasonable about the rule?

How could we resolve these problems without continual battles?

Should there be compromises?

What could you do to convince us that the rules should be changed?

What should the consequences be if the rules are broken?

Brainstorm: We could examine the family rules and the reasons for them. We could discuss how the rules should be applied and we could agree on a set of consequences if they are broken. (Remember to involve your child in the brainstorming process!)

Select: Let's write down a list of the rules so that you will know what's acceptable and unacceptable. You can refer to the list if you have any questions.

★ ★ ★ ★

Define Problem: Your grades have begun to slip. (Alternative: You seem to be spending very little time doing your homework.)

Investigate Issues:

Are you concerned?

I'm curious about why you think this is happening.

Do you need a tutor?

Do you feel you are spending enough time on your studies?

Do you see any solutions to the problem? How can we help?

Tell me your specific goals for this semester.

Would it be beneficial to set up a conference with your teachers and your counselor?

What are the potential consequences if you do not improve your grades?

Brainstorm: You could list each of your courses and list any specific problem areas. You could then establish target grades in each course, and you could indicate how much time would be required to reach the targets.

Select: You might tape your "Target List" above your desk and begin checking off each objective you achieve.

★ ★ ★ ★

58

Define Problem: You and your younger brother are fighting too much and the fighting is creating a great deal of stress in the family.

Investigate Issues:

Do you enjoy fighting with your brother?

I'm curious about what causes the fights.

Are there ways to deal with the issues without fighting?

I wonder if the source of the arguments could be eliminated?

What do you think your responsibilities are as the oldest child?

Can you do things to avoid the problems?

Tell me what changes you would like to see in your brother.

Would you be willing to discuss the issues with him?

I wonder how we could help you resolve the problem.

How do you think we should respond when you two are fighting?

What specific agreements can we make about how to deal with an argument if one should arise?

Brainstorm: You could set up a meeting with your brother. You could each make a list of the things that you both do that bug each other. You could then agree to change certain behaviors and even sign a contract.

Select: Both you and your brother could tape the list of behaviors above your desks. Each time there is an argument, you could check out who is responsible for the behavior that triggered the problem.

★ ★ ★ ★

The primary goal of these activities is to impress upon your child that strategic problem-solving methods can be used with a wide range of challenging situations. With guidance and practice, your child can begin to respond almost reflexively to these challenges. He will learn to define the problem, investigate the underlying issues, brainstorm solutions to the problem, and then select a way to evaluate the effectiveness of the ideas produced during the brainstorming session. Although your child may not use the DIBS System every time, he will know that the system is always there as a resource.

From time to time, you may need to remind your child to use the system when you see him floundering. Once he integrates the methods into his response patterns, the quality of his analytical thinking process will improve, and he will begin to think and act smarter.

CONVINCING YOUR CHILD THAT HE OR SHE IS SMART

Smartness is a state of mind and an attitude. The child who has acquired this state of mind is convinced that he has the ability to make things happen to his advantage. He *knows* that he can cope, survive and prevail in a competitive world.

The smart student who decides she wants to be a physician will approach strategically the challenge of getting into medical school. Although she is extremely intelligent, has a good scientific aptitude, and receives excellent grades in high school and college, she realizes in college that other equally bright and talented students will be applying for the limited number of places at the best medical schools.

To improve her chances of being admitted to the school of her choice, she formulates a strategy. During her summer break, she volunteers to work as an aide in an inner-city medical clinic. The following summer, she works as a lab assistant to a research pharmacologist. During the summer of her junior year, she works as an assistant in the social services department on an Indian reservation. At each job, she impresses her bosses with her diligence, and when she applies to medical school, she is able to provide excellent recommendations from her supervisors. To provide herself with an added advantage, she enrolls in an intensive review course before taking the medical aptitude test given in her senior year. Because she is smart, she applies to several schools that are not as prestigious as her first choices. These are her "fall-back" schools. These strategic steps all but guarantee her admission.

Two significant characteristics distinguish the student described above: she defines her goals and is confident that she can attain them. She not only figures out how to get from point A to point B, she also knows how to locate point C in the event that it becomes necessary to take a short cut or a detour. Realizing that she wants the brass ring, she accepts that she must compete with others and with herself to attain the desired prize. In reaching for the ring, she stretches herself to her limits.

Whereas some children seem to know at an early age that they can get where they want to go and are convinced that they have the ability to attain their goals, others—perhaps the majority—need help. As parents, you can play a vital role in providing this help.

The following supplemental exercises reinforce strategic decision-making. Your child's responses should be examined non-critically. Enjoy the activities! Help your child discover that learning how to think smart can be fun. If your child's responses are flawed or non-logical, discuss and examine the responses without communicating displeasure or disappointment. You might say, "That's interesting. Do you think if you saw smoke coming out of the house next door you might have . . .?" Or, "Let's look and see if that response is the best."

Supplemental Activity
MAKING SMART DECISIONS
Children ages 7-12

★ Imagine that you return from school and discover that you have lost your house key. You know that your mom and I will not be home until 6 o'clock. What could you do? Describe the different steps you would take.

★ Your sister feels dizzy and nauseous. She tells you she has a terrible headache. Mom is shopping, and I am at work. What steps would you take?

★ You smell something burning at night. Everyone is sleeping. You go to the workshop door and are about to open it when you discover that the door handle is very hot. What would you do?

★ You know that a bunch of tough kids hang out in front of a convenience store. They are the town bullies. You are on your bike and want an ice cream. What could you do?

61

★ You see a man you do not know talking to the little girl next door in front of her house. He is trying to talk the girl into coming into his car. What could you do?

★ You are having difficulty learning your spelling words for the weekly quiz. What could you do?

★ You and your friend are riding your bikes, and it starts to get dark. You know you are far from the house, and you think you may be lost. What could you do?

★ You have an afternoon paper route, and you enjoy having the extra money that you earn. You decide that you would like to join a football team that plays every afternoon. What could you do?

★ Your grades in math have been slipping. What could you do?

★ You've chosen a present that you want to buy Mom for her birthday. You don't have enough money. What are some solutions to this problem?

★ You don't seem to be getting along with your teacher. She is punishing you at least once a week. What could you do?

★ One of your friends is telling others some of the secrets you shared. What could you do?

[If more work is needed in the area of decision-making, or if you and your child are enjoying examining these types of life experiences, you can make up more scenarios. You might even ask your child to make some up so that the tables are turned and you demonstrate how you would respond.]

Supplemental Activity
MAKING SMART DECISIONS
Teenagers ages 13-17

★ You need $200 for the prom to cover renting a tux, food, a corsage and the other expenses. You don't have enough money. What could you do?

★   You like a particular girl (or boy), but she doesn't seem to be aware that you exist. What could you do?

★   You would like to have a party, but Dad and I are concerned that the kids will wreck the house and have said "no" to the idea. What could you do?

★   You have gone to a party with a friend in his car. At the party, he drinks a lot of beer. He seems drunk. What would you do when it is time to leave?

★   You know that you will need recommendations from your teachers when you apply to college in 6 months. What could you do?

★   You are having problems in Spanish and feel that you are hopelessly behind. What could you do?

★   It's late at night. You are alone in the car on an isolated stretch of road, and the engine stalls. You can't get it started. What would you do?

★   We are upset about your last report card. We feel you can do better, and we won't let you use the car until your grades improve. What could you do?

★   You are sick and miss a week of school. When you return to school, you discover that you have a great deal of work to do if you are to catch up. What could you do?

★   Your best friend asks you to help her cheat on an exam. You don't want to, but you are afraid that she will be angry at you. What could you do?

★   You discover that some kids are planning to put some drugs in the punch at a party. What would you do?

Chapter 3
Strategic Introspection

SHE HAD TO BE IN CHARGE

The ritual is predictable. At precisely 3:15, the back door slams, and the school books are dropped on the table in the hall. From there Blair goes to the kitchen, has some cookies and milk, and retreats to her room to read and play with her cat until dinnertime. An only child, the 11-year-old is bright, articulate, and far more comfortable talking with her parents' friends than she is interacting with children her own age. Because of her poise with adults, they invariably describe the sixth-grader as "remarkably mature for her age."

When Blair does play with other children, she usually chooses younger children whom she can "mother" or boss. On those rare occasions when a classmate visits, the guest quickly discovers that Blair expects to be in charge. She is willing to do only those things that interest her and insists that everything be done her way. If the visitor disagrees with her plan, Blair's standard response is to retreat to her room to read. Classmates rarely return for a second visit.

When asked by her parents why she spends so much time alone, Blair tells them that children her age are silly and that she prefers to read or play with younger children because they are cute. Despite her seeming indifference to her social isolation, Blair's parents know that she is deeply hurt when she is not invited to birthday parties and outings. They share her pain.

CHOOSING THE RIGHT PATH

Children arrive at many crossroads in their lives. Some paths point toward achievement and self-fulfillment. Others point toward painful collisions with reality. Because parents have faced similar crossroads in their own lives, most recognize how critically important their child's choices at these junctures can be. The future course of the child's life may hang in the balance.

A child at a crossroad may find herself pulled by powerful and seemingly mysterious forces down one path or another. At the age of 7, she may choose to become a concert violinist and may dedicate her life to attaining her goal. Or, at the age of 7, she may make an unconscious choice to sabotage herself, and her life from this point on will become a series of self-defeating decisions and actions guaranteed to produce failure.

When Blair faced the crossroad, she chose a path that led toward increasing social isolation and unhappiness. Had she proceeded too far down this path, she might never have been able to retrace her steps.

Although the forces that pull a child in one direction or another are complex, they are not all that mysterious. Primary factors affecting a child's choices, reactions and behavior include:

★ inherited characteristics and abilities
★ home environment
★ educational experiences
★ life experiences
★ cultural experiences

The universal desire of all responsible parents is to help their child become happy, well-adjusted and self-actualized. Translating this desire into reality and learning how to point the child in a direction that leads to self-actualization can be a major challenge, especially if a child seems to be headed in a perilous direction.

Fortunately, parents *can* intervene when they conclude that their child is making flawed choices. The first step in this intervention process is for them to examine their child's response patterns. As they evaluate specific behaviors, a profile should emerge. They should be able to determine if their child is impetuous, irresponsible or disorganized. They should also be able to identify patterns of procrastination, blaming, giving up, manipulation or self-sabotage.

Once parents have evaluated their child's behavior, they must help him examine those behaviors that are counterproductive. Parents who encour-

65

age self-assessment are providing their child with a "compass" that he can use when he is lost, confused or stymied. This compass can help the child work his way around life's obstacles and can point him in the right direction when he finds himself at one of life's critical crossroads.

NOT GETTING HIT ON THE HEAD

Juggling feelings, thoughts, and actions demands psychological agility. Because children are rarely trained to perform this delicate balancing act, many have great difficulty handling the variables. Like Blair, they may not know how to throw the pins in the air so that they can be properly controlled. If their timing, judgment and dexterity are "off," they are in danger of getting hit by the pins when they fall.

As all parents know from personal experience, a child's response patterns can sometimes be endearing and sometimes infuriating. A toddler, for example, may see a new toy. He smiles as he reaches for it. Instant joy is produced. The sequence of events is direct and predictable. If, however, another child should see the toy and reach for it at the same time, the first child's response might be quite different. Although it is possible that he would be willing to share his toy, there is a good chance that he will assert his territorial rights and react aggressively.

The child who is responding to stimuli is crossing a "bridge" that links his actions and reactions with his underlying feelings and thoughts. Depending on the circumstances and upon the child's history, this crossing may be direct and unobstructed, or circuitous and impeded.

Imagine a 5-year-old being offered an ice cream cone and smiling in appreciation and in anticipation of pleasure. In this instance, the child is crossing the bridge on a clear day. If the same child is asked by his parents to behave at the dinner table and throws a temper tantrum, he is crossing on a foggy day. This response might be atypical and could simply indicate that the child is sleepy, cranky or sick. However, if this is the child's standard reaction to being reprimanded, it suggests that he has not yet completed the testing stage normally associated with 2-year-olds.

The nature of a child's responses is a primary indication of not only his emotional development, but also his Smartness Quotient. For example, a child may be taunted by the class bully on his way home from school. He has several response options. He could strike back, and in so doing, set the stage for a fight. Or he could decide to walk away and try to avoid a confrontation.

Because they often act and react without conscious thought and tend to respond reflexively to stimuli, children are rarely aware that they have crossed the "bridge." Their spontaneous reactions have the potential to create innumerable crises. In this respect, children are no different from their adult counterparts who become incensed when cut off on the freeway. Although a child's anger can be therapeutic, it can also be destructive when it is excessive or irrational. The child who becomes enraged when he is teased is signaling non-adaptive behavior with potentially serious implications. If he typically responds in this way, he will probably experience monumental social and vocational problems throughout his life.

Of course, a child cannot be expected to respond strategically under all circumstances. One of the "rights" of childhood is permission to be spontaneous, silly and even naughty. Certain situations, however, clearly demand measured reactions from children. For example, a smart child will realize that he cannot simply turn around and hit a child who is disturbing him in class. To do so would cause him to be even more victimized by the other child's misbehavior.

Although smart kids do not consciously analyze every response, they recognize when they are stuck, and they are willing to work at getting unstuck. The thinking child examines what is happening to him, and this self-assessment process distinguishes him from the non-thinking child.

A smart child being taunted by a bully would try to figure out what he needs to do to resolve the problem. He has several options:

★ He can avoid the bully.
★ He can seek the protection of a tough friend or a group of friends.
★ He can try to win over the bully.
★ He can decide to confront the bully.
★ He can choose to examine what he might be doing that is encouraging the bully to pick on him.

Recognizing that he must find a means to neutralize his antagonist, the smart child would assess his options and select the most advantageous strategy. In many instances, the child with a highly developed Smartness Quotient will know intuitively which option is best and will almost instantaneously choose the best response. Most children, however, need guidance and practice before they develop these smart-thinking "reflexes."

Obviously, even the smart child does not respond perfectly under all circumstances. If he is excited, upset, or simply "out of synch," he may act unreasonably. The child's normal problem-solving orientation, however, usually permits him to re-establish the delicate balance between his emotions and his actions. When he experiences a crisis or a thinking lapse, he can ultimately sort things out and "land on his feet."

The not-so-smart child has great difficulty figuring out how to coordinate his emotions and his intellect. Because he tends to respond non-strategically to stimuli, he often appears to be the victim of circumstances. Such a child is invariably the one the teacher "catches" acting out in class and the one who argues that he didn't hear the teacher announce the exam for Friday.

A child who is unable to take charge of his life may respond by resigning himself to his victim role. On the surface, the child may not appear to be troubled, but appearances can be deceptive. Resignation usually produces frustration and depression that the child may unconsciously repress because he does not want to deal with them. When asked about how things are going, he may simply respond "fine."

Some children react to their inability to take positive control of their lives by becoming mindlessly aggressive. This behavior typically precipitates recurring crises and failure that undermine the child's self-confidence. To vent his frustration, the child may initiate fights or even resort to delinquent behavior. The net result is increasingly non-adaptive behavior and a tragic waste of human potential.

Not-so-smart children are rarely self-assessing. They do not connect their poor judgment, poor planning, and lack of awareness with the negative events in their lives. For them to make this connection, they would have to develop an awareness of cause and effect, and they would have to be willing to examine their actions and reactions. (Specific methods that encourage your child to develop this awareness are presented later in this chapter.)

BREAKING NEGATIVE CYCLES

When parents conclude that their child is not thinking smart, they have several options to help him break out of this self-defeating cycle. The first option involves modifying the child's behavior with systematic feedback, praise and punishment. This methodology is called *behavior modification,* and the parents' responses to the child's negative behavior are called reinforcements.

The positive effects of behavior modification have been well-documented. As a general rule, children who are praised for newly learned behavior become increasingly "addicted" to the positive responses they are receiving from their parents and teachers. They realize that if they are to continue receiving these responses, they must be willing to change their old behavior.

For example, behavior-modification could prove quite effective in reorienting a chronically untidy child. The first step in setting up the system would be for parents and child to agree on specific behavioral objectives for the child that might include:

* making the bed each morning
* placing all dirty clothes in the hamper
* hanging up or folding and putting away all clothes that are not being used.

The desired changes in behavior would be linked to a system of reinforcements, rewards and incentives. For example, the child might receive:

* 5 points each day for making the bed
* 5 points for putting dirty clothes in the hamper
* 5 points for hanging, folding and storing unused clothes.

The "trade-in value" of the points would have to be determined by the parents, ideally with the child's participation. For instance, a predetermined number of points might earn the child the right to go to a movie with his friends on the weekend or to extend his bedtime on Friday or Saturday night. The child would also have the option of saving up his points and could apply them to earning a specific reward such as a bicycle.

As the child begins to change his behavior, he will need ongoing verbal praise, encouragement and acknowledgment in addition to points. Upon attaining the agreed-upon behavioral changes each day, the child would receive his reward in the form of points and acknowledgment. If he temporarily reverts to his previous behavior, he would be negatively reinforced by the withholding of praise and points. Some behavior-modification programs go one step further. These programs advocate not only withholding the positive reinforcement but also providing actual punishment in the form of withdrawing previously earned privileges.

Although behavior modification can be quite effective, the approach is not universally successful. Potential drawbacks include:

* The method must be applied carefully, skillfully and consistently.
* The system may become less effective as the child becomes habituated to the reinforcement techniques.
* Behavior modification can be a burden for parents who must continually monitor their child and consistently respond in a way that may

begin to seem artifical and contrived.
* Insecure children with significant psychological problems may be very resistant to changing their behavior. If the negative behavior is symptomatic of underlying problems, it is probably enmeshed in the child's personality. The child may be addicted to the negative payoffs that his counterproductive behavior elicits. Frightened, angry and unhappy children are especially resistant to change. Modifying their behavior without making inroads into the source of their despair does not necessarily produce happiness.

Parents have been using behavior modification with their children since the beginning of time. Whenever they punish or praise their child, they are modifying behavior. Despite potential shortcomings, well-conceived, systematic behavior-modification programs have proven especially effective in reorienting such counterproductive traits as irresponsibility, procrastination and sloppiness.

FUEL INJECTORS AND TURBOCHARGERS

Incorporating introspection into the previously described DIBS System (Define the problem, Investigate the issues, Brainstorm solutions, Select an idea to test) is the equivalent of adding a "fuel injector" to the child's problem-solving system. This expanded system is modeled in the following sections.

By encouraging your child to examine his behavior and the consequences of his choices, you are helping him achieve valuable insight. This insight can be a powerful stimulus for positive change and is especially important in the cases of children who are enmeshed in cycles of counterproductive behavior. The alternative is to permit the behavior to persist. This would significantly increase the risk of damaging your child's self-esteem and self-confidence.

By integrating the best features of behavior modification, introspection and strategic problem-solving, parents can create a powerful system for orienting their child toward smart thinking and effective problem-solving. In so doing, they can "turbocharge" the system. Ways to integrate these three techniques are also modeled later in this chapter.

FOUR OPTIONS FOR BREAKING NEGATIVE CYCLES

I.	II.	III.	IV.
Analytical Problem- Solving (Guided Dialogues and/or DIBS System)	Analytical Problem Solving + Introspection	Behavior Modification	Analytical Problem Solving + Introspection + Behavior Modification

THE SELF-EXAMINING CHILD

Purposeful introspection permits a child to examine the emotional terrain on the other side of the bridge that links his actions and emotions. Like their adult counterparts, children tend to resist looking at feelings they sense are unpleasant.

This aversion to self-examination is especially problematical in the case of the not-so-smart child and can cause him to become "stuck." Because the stuck child does not understand the relationship between his emotions, his actions and the consequences of his actions, he usually feels powerless to get what he wants and to extricate himself from his counterproductive system. For example, he may not connect his difficulty making friends with the fact that he is acting inappropriately in class or on the playground. Or he may not link his poor academic performance in school with the fact that he is not spending enough time studying.

The parents of a stuck child would understandably feel a strong temptation to help their child resolve his problem. It is important, however, that such parents distinguish between *helping* their child and *resolving* the problem for him. Blair's parents (the child described at the beginning of this chapter) might have asked their friends to send their children over to play with their daughter. They might have also insisted that Blair join the Girl Scouts or a gymnastics team. Another option would have been to give her feedback about how she was relating to other children and recommendations about how she might improve her social skills. Although all of these ideas make sense, they do not actively involve Blair in the process of identifying, acknowledging and figuring out how to resolve her problem. Given the nature of Blair's defense mechanisms, she would undoubtedly deny that she even had a problem.

71

Under the appropriate circumstances, crisis intervention and suggestions are justifiable. However, there is a hazard when parental intervention is habitual and conforms to a "rescue script." In Blair's case, the immediate goal was to help her become more socially competent. The long-term goal was to help her become a self-actualized and self-reliant adult. To have taken ownership of her problems would have discouraged her from taking responsibility for identifying, examining and resolving her own problems. Clearly, Blair required parental assistance. At issue was how best to provide this assistance.

One option for redirecting Blair's non-adaptive social behavior would have been for her parents to set up a behavior-modification system. With positive feedback and encouragement—and hopefully with increasingly positive reactions of other children—Blair might have altered her style of relating to other children.

Behavior modification might have reduced Blair's social difficulties, but it would not have necessarily changed her underlying negative feelings about herself. Despite outward changes, these feelings might have begun to manifest themselves in other self-defeating forms. Encouraging Blair to develop behaviors that would make her more socially acceptable could have produced some immediate benefits. In the long run, however, encouraging her to examine her underlying feelings and helping her discover through brainstorming more effective ways to relate to children probably would have proven more beneficial.

Combining introspection and behavior modification offers many distinct advantages over either system if used alone. This approach is modeled in the dialogue on the opposite page.

Parents who observe that their child is not responding to their efforts to reorient self-defeating behavior patterns are strongly advised to have their child professionally assessed by a mental-health specialist. Children with serious, entrenched counterproductive behavior patterns and/or emotional problems should be evaluated and treated professionally.

A MODEL FOR INTROSPECTIVE PROBLEM-SOLVING

In the following dialogue, Blair's mother guides her daughter toward a greater awareness of her actions and behavior. She shows her how she can monitor her own behavior, and she provides her feedback and support for changing counterproductive behavior.

You will note that although the parent participates in the process of helping the child examine her actions and feelings, she is careful not to take responsibility for solving the problem. She realizes that her primary

72

role is to guide her daughter through the self-assessment/problem-solving process.

Model Dialogue #4
INTROSPECTIVE PROBLEM-SOLVING
Children ages 7-12

Parent: Honey, I sense that you are upset because you do not have as many friends as you would like.

Child: I don't care.

Parent: You don't care about not having friends and not being invited to parties?

Child: No.

Parent: No?

Child: I don't care if kids don't like me.

Parent: Tell me why kids don't like you.

Child: I don't know.

Parent: Is there something you're doing that might be turning kids off? Can you think of anything?

Child: No.

Parent: Sometimes I've watched you play with children who come over to the house. I've observed that you tend to order them around. They always have to do what you want to do. Am I right?

Child: Maybe.

Parent: Do you think kids like taking orders from their friends?

Child: Probably not.

Parent: I know I wouldn't like it if I went to someone's house to visit, and she ordered me around and insisted that we only do the things she wanted to do. Would you be willing to try an experiment?

Child: What do you mean?

Parent: By an experiment I mean that you'll try something and see if it corrects a problem. Do you have any ideas about how to solve your problem?

73

Child:	I could try not to boss them.
Parent:	That makes a lot of sense. Let's see how you could actually set up an experiment about bossing kids around. Where could you start?
Child:	I don't know.
Parent:	How about making a two-column checklist? One column you could call "Giving Orders." The second column you could call "Deciding Together." Invite a friend over next Saturday. As you play together, you could keep track in your mind of how many times you make decisions about what to do and how many times your friend makes the choices. After she leaves, mark down the number in each column. You could do the experiment for a month and see if you get better at letting other people participate in making decisions. How does the experiment sound?
Child:	Good.
Parent:	Super! We'll take a look at the chart from time to time to make sure it's being filled out correctly. Okay?
Child:	Okay.

The mother in the preceding dialogue clearly has a strategy in mind before beginning the discussion. Her goals are to help her daughter achieve insight and to modify specific counterproductive behaviors. She allows the insights and ideas to evolve during the brainstorming session. In so doing, she makes deriving the solution a collective effort.

You cannot be certain what will happen during a discussion with your child. Sometimes, your child will need only a little help figuring out her own solution to the problem. In other instances, you will have to guide your child patiently toward achieving the insight that will permit her to solve the problem. Ideally, the solution will evolve as a result of you and your child "putting your heads together." Be forewarned that there will be false starts, and ideas may prove unworkable. Sometimes, no ideas will emerge from the discussion, and several attempts at brainstorming may be necessary. The discussion may also take unexpected turns, and no amount of preparation can totally prepare you for these detours. Nevertheless, you should think about solution-oriented strategies in advance, especially when working with a child who is shy or non-communicative.

PROBLEM-MANAGEMENT CHECKLIST

A child's willingness to look at his behavior, actions and responses to challenges and dilemmas is a key to developing effective problem-management skills. The child who learns how to manage problems effectively can begin to assert positive control over his life.

The following checklist is designed to help you assess your child's current problem-managing attitudes and skills. Later in the chapter, you will find a similar checklist for your child to complete. This checklist is intended to encourage your child to examine his or her responses to problems. A final checklist can be found in the concluding chapter of the book. The parent checklist and the "before" and "after" checklists will permit you and your child to gauge changes in behavior and performance.

Checklist for Parent ## *PROBLEM-MANAGEMENT*

Code: 0 = Never 1 = Rarely 2 — Sometimes
     3 = Often 4 = Always

My child tends to avoid confronting problems or challenges. _____

My child insists on getting his or her own way, even if it is not working. _____

My child is unwilling to accept suggestions and help. _____

My child gets upset when frustrated. _____

My child cannot think clearly when upset or frustrated. _____

My child gives up easily. _____

My child has difficulty developing strategies for solving problems. _____

My child is disorganized. _____

My child tends to blame others for his or her problems. _____

My child is passive. _____

My child easily accepts that problems are   _____
insurmountable.

My child tends to repeat the same mistakes.   _____

My child becomes defensive when a problem is   _____
pointed out.

My child procrastinates when faced with a   _____
challenge, problem or a chore.

My child denies that he or she has problems that   _____
must be resolved.

TOTAL   _____

Interpreting the Checklist

A pattern of 3's and 4's suggests that your child is having difficulty managing problems and challenges. If the total points exceed 30, the following experiments and supplemental activities are especially important.

INTRODUCING THE PROBLEM-MANAGEMENT CHECKLIST

It would now be advisable for your child to complete the problem-management checklist for children. Although this checklist can be used with children of all ages, younger children will probably require parental assistance to help them understand some of the statements and issues. Before your child begins, emphasize that the checklist is not a test, but simply part of a smart-thinking program that you and he or she are examining together. You might say: "I'm enjoying doing these experiments with you, and I hope you are also enjoying doing them. Before we do the next activity, I'd like you to complete this checklist."

You may wish to discuss your child's responses after the checklist is completed, or you may wish to do so at a later date. Discussion *while* your child is completing the checklist, however, could inhibit your child and influence his or her responses. When you do discuss the responses, be careful not to slip into a parent-sermon mode. Remember, you are advocating that your child develop the capacity to use introspection as a problem-solving resource. Consequently, you also have a responsibility to be self-assessing. If you recognize in yourself a tendency to lecture or preach, you will need to do some personal brainstorming about how you might resist this tendency *before* discussing the checklist with your child.

Checklist for Child
MANAGING PROBLEMS

Code: 0 = Never   1 = Rarely
   2 = Sometimes   3 = Often   4 = Always

I avoid trying to solve problems. _____

I insist on getting my own way, even if it is not working. _____

I am not willing to accept suggestions and help. _____

I get upset when I become frustrated. _____

I have difficulty doing something when I am upset or frustrated. _____

I give up when a job is difficult. _____

I have difficulty figuring out how to solve problems. _____

I do not have the materials I need to do the job. _____

I blame others for my problems. _____

I make the same mistakes over and over. _____

I don't like it when someone points out a problem. _____

I tend to put off dealing with problems or chores. _____

I don't like to admit that there is a problem or challenge that I need to deal with. _____

TOTAL _____

Discussing the Checklist With Your Child

Make a note of your child's total score, but be careful not to make your child feel that he is being tested. Explain to your child that the score is added up to permit a comparison at a later date when he will complete the same checklist once again. If it "feels right," you may want to use the checklist at this time to initiate a discussion about some of the issues that are covered. Remind your child that the second checklist will help you both determine if there have been any changes as a result of doing the activities in the book.

ALTERNATIVE STRATEGIES

A wide range of approaches can be effective in helping a child examine his or her behavior. For instance, Blair's mother might have used a different approach than the one modeled in the dialogue. She might have begun the examination process by asking: "Do you think it's important to be popular?" Or she could have begun: "I suppose kids feel it's real important to be popular." Using the "third person" can be less threatening than a direct question or statement, and this technique can be especially effective with children who are shy, insecure, defensive or reluctant to express feelings (e.g., "If a child felt he were unpopular, could he do things to make himself more popular?").

As you work with your child on problems, alternate the use of questions and statements. Be prepared to listen actively, supportively, and non-judgmentally. Avoid giving your child "the third degree." When your child expresses a feeling or idea, you might simply respond: "That's interesting." Or you might say: "Have you ever considered . . . ?"

The DIBS System presented in Chapter 2 is an alternative to the dialogue method. Its objective is the same: to help your child attain insight into his thinking, feelings and behavior. The DIBS System can be even more effective when it incorporates self-assessment and introspection. Below, you will find this expanded DIBS System applied to some typical problem situations. Note that introspection is encouraged during the I (Investigation) phase. Before introducing the expanded system, it would be appropriate to review with your child the components of the method (see page 49). You might also explain that everyone in the family is going to be encouraged to use the system whenever there is a problem and that to use the system properly, everyone needs to practice.

Keep the DIBS sessions relatively short, especially in the case of younger children. Remember that a child's attention span is shorter than yours. You might want to examine only one of the problems at a time. By extending the sessions over several days, you are giving your child a chance to master the system and sort out his feelings. Don't expect that a problem will necessarily be resolved each time you and your child apply the DIBS System. Your child will need time to assimilate the insights, and he will require practice before he can reasonably be expected to master the method.

One final observation about the tone of the DIBS sessions modeled below. You will note that the issues covered during the investigation/introspection phase are frequently raised as questions. Although questions should be asked, they should be balanced with statements. For example, you might say: "I suppose it's important for a child to be popular." This is an effective alternative to: "Is it important to be popular?" You might also say: "From things you've said, I gather that it's real important for kids to be popular." As has been previously stated, avoid bombarding your child with questions and try to alternate questions and statements.

Do not feel that you must examine all, or even most, of the many issues that are raised below. More issues are raised than need to be discussed. If your child actively participates in examining just one or two issues, he will benefit far more than by participating passively in a drawn-out discussion of twenty issues. Also feel free to substitute other situations that are more relevant to you and your child.

Read the material modeled below *before* you attempt to explore the problems and issues with your child. Make mental notes about what you'd like to explore. You are advised, however, not to take written notes during the discussion. Your child would probably find this inhibiting.

Do not feel bound by an agenda. What is important is that your child have an opportunity to develop and practice a new skill. As he becomes increasingly comfortable with the analytical/introspective process, he should begin to respond more strategically to challenges and problems.

Don't be surprised if your discussion with your child takes a very different tack from the one described below. Go with the flow of the discussion, and do not feel that you must control the conversation in order to cover the issues presented in the model. Be especially sensitive to when it's time to stop!

Allow sufficient time for your child to think about and respond to the issues raised. You may have to modify the language if you are communicating with a younger child. Remember to use vocabulary that your child can understand and select topics that are relevant to your child.

You will note that the subject being explored in the following application of the expanded DIBS System contains several overlapping issues. By showing your child how to define each issue and how to apply the investigation/introspection method to exploring the issue, you are helping him learn to identify, sort out and systematically evaluate a subject that might otherwise appear complex and overwhelming. This divide-and-conquer concept is central to the development of analytical thinking skills.

The DIBS System
THINKING AND INTROSPECTION
Children and Teenagers ages 7-17

Problem:

Imagine that you know a child in school who doesn't have as many friends as she would like. Let's look at how she (he) might deal with this problem. You remember that the first step in solving a problem is to define or identify the problem. Do we agree that the child's problem is that she doesn't have enough friends? Now that the problem is defined, the next step is to examine some of the issues involved in the problem. We'll do that together. Let's see how many issues we can find. I have some in mind, and we can examine them together. You think about issues that come to your mind. I'll start, and you interrupt at any time with your ideas.

Define (Issue):

Let's look at this issue first. Why do you think it's important to be popular?

**Investigation/
Introspection:**

I wonder why people need to be liked. Do you think being accepted is important only to kids, or do adults also need to be liked and accepted? Does a child need to be popular in order to be happy? I wonder if a child needs to be happy in order to be popular.

Define (Issue):

I'm curious about what makes kids popular.

**Investigation/
Introspection:**

I suppose a child would have to do what the other kids were doing to be accepted. Is this true? I wonder if a child could think and act differently without being considered weird. Could you like a child who acted differently from other kids if the child was nice? Do only the popular kids become leaders? Tell me what makes kids leaders.

80

Define (Issue):	What makes kids unpopular?
Investigation/ Introspection:	How would an unpopular kid feel? Could a child who is unpopular still have some friends? Would having just one or two friends be enough? Does the unpopular child want to be liked by everyone? Tell me what's different about the behavior of unpopular kids.
Define (Issue):	I wonder how an unpopular child could find out what was causing him to be unpopular.
Investigation/ Introspection:	I'm curious about how someone could find out what "turns people off." How can we get feedback about our behavior? By this I mean how can we find out how people are feeling about our behavior? How can we check out if this feedback is accurate?
Define (Issue):	Let's assume a child concluded he was unpopular. Do you think it would help if he changed his behavior?
Investigation/ Introspection:	Do you think that if a child changes his unacceptable behavior, he would be more popular? I wonder what would happen if someone decides to "be himself" no matter what. When we change our behavior, do we become different people? Could someone study the behavior of popular kids and try to be like them? Can a child intentionally do things that will make him more popular?
Brainstorming:	I recall that last week you told me you wished you had more friends. In the light of what we have just discussed, let's see if we can brainstorm some solutions to this problem. Do you have any ideas? How about making up a list of the things you could possibly do to make more friends? Let's see if we

81

can take these ideas and set up an experiment so that you can measure whether or not the strategy is successful? Do you think you could make up some sort of chart that would allow you to keep track of whether you are making the changes in your behavior that you want to make. You could also keep track of whether the changes are having any effect. (See next sections for facsimiles of different types of charts.)

Select: How about starting to use the chart tomorrow? If you'd like we can take a look at the chart every Friday and discuss the progress you are making.

The parent who learns how to help a child identify underlying issues and brainstorm solutions to problems has acquired an important parenting skill. At first, this process of helping your child develop insight can be challenging. Some suggestions are in order. Make the DIBS sessions enjoyable! Be creative. And above all, be supportive and positive. As your child becomes more competent, he will begin to internalize the method.

Be forewarned that the DIBS System can backfire. If you make the process a drudgery, your child will resist using it. The keys to making the system work are:

★ *Use it selectively.* (If you are constantly insisting that your child use the system, you will trigger resistance.)
★ *Plan ahead.* (Think about the issues and possible solutions before you meet with your child. If you reach an impasse, be prepared to stimulate the brainstorming session.)
★ *Don't give sermons.*
★ *Don't be judgmental.*
★ *Provide lots of support and encouragement.*

MONITORING ACTIVITIES AND EXERCISES

Helping your child learn how to think smart may require significant changes in his or her attitude and behavior. Before this is possible, you and your child must define and agree upon the desired changes. The next step is to devise a system for monitoring the changes. (Techniques for establishing short and long-term goals will be examined in depth in the next chapter.)

82

The following scenarios provide more examples of how the DIBS System can be used to examine and resolve typical problems. Once you have completed the brainstorming session, you and your child can create an appropriate monitoring system. You may sense intuitively that a reward should be integrated into this system. For example, you might say: "If the monitoring system indicates that you have achieved the objective, I propose to . . . as a reward."

When you combine the DIBS System with a mutually acceptable method for gauging change, you reduce the likelihood of parent-child showdowns. Encourage your child to make suggestions about what categories will be included in the monitoring system (see sample chart on page 84). His or her active involvement will significantly increase the effectiveness of the procedure. Remember, it is vital that you enthusiastically acknowledge and affirm your child when he or she makes positive changes in behavior!

The DIBS System
ENCOURAGING INTROSPECTION
Children ages 7-12

Problem:	A child realizes he has developed the habit of exaggerating and sometimes telling lies. He has gotten "caught" several times by his parents and teacher and was very embarrassed.
Define (Issue):	Do you think lying can sometimes be justified?
Investigation/ Introspection:	What are the consequences of lying? Can lying cause a child to be unhappy? Tell me if you think the child who lies should be punished.
Define (Issue):	I wonder what could cause a child to lie.
Investigation/ Introspection:	Does a child need to lie in order to be liked? Does he lie to impress other children? Do you suppose that he lies because he feels that he isn't good enough?
Define (Issue):	I wonder if lying is making the child happy.

Investigation/
Introspection: Does it ever make sense to lie? Do smart kids lie? Do you think other children know when a child is lying? Do you think his parents know when he is lying? Does the teacher know when he is lying? Tell me why smart kids would not want to lie. Is it reasonable for his parents, teachers and friends to be upset by his lying? How do you think they would respond?

Define (Issue): I wonder if the child could change his behavior.

Investigation/
Introspection: Would he want to change? I wonder if being more truthful would make him happier. Could he be popular if he didn't lie?

Brainstorming: I bet that if the child wanted to change his behavior, he could design a system for checking himself. At the end of the day, he could write down the number of times he told a lie, the number of times he told

SELF-MONITORING CHART

Day	EXAGGERATED	TOLD TRUTH	TOLD LIE
Monday:			
Tuesday:			
Wednesday:			
Thursday:			
Friday:			
Saturday:			
Sunday:			
Weekly Total:			

the truth and the number of times he resisted the temptation to lie or exaggerate. In this way he could keep track and would know if his behavior was changing. The chart might look like this (see opposite page):

Select: The child could use the chart and review his progress each week.

★ ★ ★ ★

Problem: You have told us that Mom and I are being unfair for getting on your case about not keeping your room neat. I sense that you are becoming angry at us.

Define (Issue):   Do you think parents have a right to be concerned about whether their child's room is neat or not?

**Investigation/
Introspection:**   Why would parents be concerned if their child's room was sloppy or dirty? Do kids "own" their rooms? Do parents have a right to insist on a minimum standard of neatness and cleanliness? How could kids and parents determine a fair standard of neatness? Tell me how parents should monitor their child's room. What can kids do if they feel their parents are being unfair?

Brainstorming: Let's make up a list of your "rights" and our "rights." Then let's agree to some reasonable standards. We'll create a system that allows us to know if your room meets the agreed-upon standard. In this way, we would not have to be constantly reminding you. We could also combine a reward system with the monitoring system. If you feel that you have met the standard, you will put a check in each column on the chart. If we agree that you have met the standard, you might earn points toward a new .... The chart might look like this:

MY RESPONSIBILITIES AT HOME

CATEGORY	Mon.	Tue.	Wed.	Thu.	Fri.	Sat.	Sun
Clothes put away							
Bed made							
Dirty clothes in hamper							
Things put away							
Add item*							
Add item*							
Add item*							

Select: Would you want to begin using the chart tomorrow? We could meet each week to discuss your progress.

The DIBS System
ENCOURAGING INTROSPECTION
Teenagers ages 13-17

Problem: Several times each week either your Dad or I have to remind you about doing your homework. You resent that we are hassling you, and we resent that you are not doing your homework without us having to remind you.

Define (Issue): Do you feel parents have a "right" to be concerned about their teenager's schoolwork?

Investigation Introspection: Do you think it is reasonable to expect that a minimum amount of homework be done each evening? Who should determine what is a reasonable amount? I wonder how you could establish a reasonable homework formula. If there are disagreements, how should they be handled?

Define (Issue): What can and should parents do if their child's grades begin to slide?

Investigation/ Introspection: How should parents express their concerns? How could parents and kids avoid showdowns and resentment about the subject of homework and grades? I wonder if there are ways for us to avoid pressing each other's "hot buttons" when the issue of school is discussed.

Brainstorming: Let's see if we can agree on a reasonable homework/ studying formula that is fair and reasonable and that will avoid arguments. Then let's set up a system that permits *you* to monitor your study time and your performance. You might also build into the monitoring system a way to compare your grades before you started using the system and your grades after you begin using the system. How much time do you feel you need to spend each evening in your subjects?

History _____

Math _____

English _____

French _____

Science _____

Once we agree on a reasonable formula, you can use a chart for keeping track of your study time and the grades you receive. After each subject, you could write the number of minutes agreed upon. You could then make a slash and write the number of minutes actually spent studying on that day. (See

87

the next chapter for a more comprehensive examination of time management.)

HOURS SPENT STUDYING EACH EVENING

Subject	Mon.	Tue.	Wed.	Thu.	Fri.	Sat.	Sun.	Current Grade
History	*/**							
Math								
English								
French								
Science								
Projects								
TOTALS								

* estimated time
** actual time spent

Select: Would you want to begin using the chart tomorrow? We could discuss your progress each week.

Problem: Your last report card indicated that your grades have slipped. As you well know, Mom and I grounded you and forbade you to use your car for social purposes. You have told us that you feel we are being unfair. We can see that you are upset with us.

Define (Issue): Do you feel that parents have the right to insist on a standard of performance?

Investigation/ Introspection: I'm curious about what makes a performance standard fair or unfair? Should parents take away privileges if a child does not meet the standard? Is having access to a car a privilege for a teenager or a right? I wonder how we as a family might arrive at a fair standard of performance and agree on reasonable consequences for non-performance or laziness. How should parents express their concern or dissatisfaction about their child's performance? Should there be consequences for poor performance in school?

Define (Issue):   Why are grades important?

Investigation/ Introspection:

What purpose do grades have? Tell me who might ultimately want to see your grades besides you and us. What would good grades indicate? What would poor grades indicate? I wonder if a student's grades indicate something about his or her level of pride, effort and sense of responsibility. Tell me what your responsibilities are regarding schoolwork? I'm curious about what you think our responsibilities should be as far as monitoring your effort and your work? If an academic problem develops, how should it be handled by you and by us? How could the present problem best be solved?

Brainstorming:

To avoid confrontations, perhaps you could keep track of your own school performance. In this way, you will know if your work falls off. If your grades should drop, we could then examine options for identifying and correcting the problem. These options could range from increasing study time to finding a tutor. Let's see if we can design a chart for keeping track of your grades on quizzes, exams, reports, essays, etc. (*Note:* The following chart deals exclusively with performance and does not include the actual amount of time the student spends studying.)

WEEKLY PERFORMANCE
(Grades on Quizzes, Exams, Reports, Essays)

SUBJECT	Mar. 1-6	Mar. 9-13	Mar. 16-20	Mar. 23-27
History				
Math				
English				
French				
Science				

Select: Would you want to begin using the performance chart this week? We could meet each week to discuss your progress.

THE "TOO-SMART" CHILD

Like any skill or resource, smartness must be used wisely by a child. No parent wants her 10-year-old to become so strategic that he begins to scheme. The child who becomes "too smart for his own good" can be carried away by his own power to get what he wants and to make things happen to his advantage. Such a child is at risk for becoming manipulative, self-centered and conniving. He may decide that cutting corners is the only way to win. If the child loses perspective, cuts too many corners, and concludes that winning at all costs is acceptable, he could easily cross the line that separates honesty from dishonesty.

Although it is clearly desirable that a child learn how to think smart and how to establish goals, it is also desirable that he develop a value system and a sense of morality. The child who rationalizes that plagiarizing a term paper is OK because the primary concern is to get a good grade is establishing an attitude destined to lead to serious problems. The same child might also rationalize that it's OK to tell half-truths when expedient or to imply that someone else is guilty of something that he has done. Later in life, he may convince himself that breaking the law is equally justifiable.

When you encourage your child to become introspective and to assess himself, you reduce the risk of him developing a "too-smart-for-his-own-good" syndrome. The process of instilling ethics must begin during early childhood and should continue throughout the formative years. *While*

90

teaching your child to be smart, you must be careful to teach him that the
ends do not always justify the means.

In some respects, learning how to think smart is like learning karate. Both skills carry great responsibility. Your child must recognize that he cannot abuse his skill. Just as his karate instructor must impress upon him that he now has the ability to injure another child, so must you impress upon your child that he now has another powerful resource—his SQ— that he must use wisely. Winning at all costs is not OK. Children who fail to appreciate this are destined to get into trouble.

Supplemental Activity
IDENTIFYING HOW PEOPLE THINK
Children ages 7-12

I would like to do a fun activity with you. The activity involves placing events into similar groups. Below is a list of things different children have done. We'll read the descriptions and decide whether the child's actions are "smart" or "not so smart." We will place a plus sign [+] in front of each smart action and a minus sign [−] by each not-so-smart action. We'll also tell our reasons for our decision. There are no right or wrong answers. If we don't agree, we'll explain why we feel the way we do.

_____ A child talks back to the teacher.

_____ She hands in her homework on time.

_____ He copies over his sloppy report.

_____ He is late for dinner three days in a row and is punished.

_____ She leaves the books she needs to study in her locker at school.

_____ He makes several errors during the baseball game on Saturday and decides to quit the Little League team.

_____ She reveals a secret her best friend told her.

_____ She spends an hour each evening practicing for her piano recital.

_____ He rides his bicycle at night without a light.

_____ She takes money from her mother's purse without telling her.

_____ He agrees to try the cigarette that his friend offers him.

_____ He pretends he is sick so that he doesn't have to go to school.

_____ She does a project for extra credit in history.

_____ He finds a wallet with money in it and returns it to the owner.

_____ She begins saving for the present she wants to buy her mom three months before her mom's birthday.

_____ Her friend falls off her bike and hurts herself, and she calls the emergency number 911.

_____ He wants to make the basketball team and he practices for an hour each day after school.

_____ He puts paper in a wastepaper basket and lights it with a match.

_____ He sees a teenager selling drugs to a kid at school and tells his parents.

_____ She refuses to approach the car of a man she doesn't know who tries to talk to her on her way home from school.

Supplemental Activity
IDENTIFYING HOW PEOPLE THINK
Teenagers ages 13-17

I feel that this process we've been going through of analyzing actions and decisions is important and valuable. Let's look at some situations and analyze them together. Once we evaluate each situation, we will decide if it is "smart thinking," "not smart thinking" or we are unsure. We will put a plus sign [+] by each smart-thinking situation, a minus sign [−] by each not-smart-thinking one, and a question mark [?] for those about which we are unsure. In this way, we can compare and contrast our thoughts about the underlying issues. There are no necessarily right or wrong answers. Some actions, however, are clearly smarter and more strategic than others. What I'm suggesting is that we examine together some life experiences. The way in which we look at these experiences and events will, of course, influence how we respond to them.

_____ She starts flirting with her boyfriend's best friend.

_____ He begins to work out seriously a couple of months before football practice starts in the fall.

_____ She cuts back on the hours she spends at her after-school job because she starts falling behind in math and English.

_____ He begins reading the assigned book immediately so that he can complete the book report in time to go on a previously planned weekend skiing trip.

_____ She decides to break off a friendship with a girl who has become addicted to drugs.

_____ He takes the family car knowing that his parents don't want him to drive it.

_____ He begins eating too many sweets, puts on 20 pounds, and is now overweight.

_____ She is confused in algebra class but is embarrassed to ask the teacher for help.

_____ He gets two speeding tickets in one week.

_____ He is unhappy with his grade on a report and makes an appointment to discuss the matter with his English teacher.

_____ She forgets to do assignments because she doesn't write them in her notebook.

_____ He refuses to drive in a car with a friend who has been drinking.

_____ She quits the volleyball team because the coach is strict and demanding.

_____ She agrees to help her best friend out of a jam and lends her $15.

_____ He drives on bald tires.

_____ He flirts with his girlfriend's best friend.

_____ He wants to win an athletic scholarship in track but refuses to stop smoking.

_____ She drives home from a party late at night when she is very sleepy.

Chapter 4
Establishing Priorities and Goals

MAKING THE STANFORD WATER POLO TEAM

When he was 8 years old, Martin knew that he wanted to follow in his dad's footsteps. His father had been a star athlete in high school who had gone to Stanford on an athletic scholarship and had played on the university's championship water polo team. Martin had visions of not only playing water polo at Stanford, but also of making the U.S. Olympic Team.

On Monday, Wednesday and Friday mornings, the 13-year-old would force himself out of bed at 5 a.m. and join his father, a competitive swimmer in the Masters Program, for early-morning swims in the San Francisco Bay. They would follow this regimen even during the winter. On Tuesday and Thursday mornings, Martin and his dad did 100 laps in the community swimming pool. Tuesday and Thursday afternoons were devoted to water polo. Martin's father would pick his son up after school and drive him to the Stanford pool. There he joined 30 other teenagers who were being trained by one of the water polo coaches.

Martin's father did not coerce his son to pursue water polo. It was the seventh-grader's decision to participate in the training program. Although the practices were long and grueling, Martin loved them. He had a plan and a goal and never doubted for a moment that the effort was worthwhile.

THE GOAL-DIRECTED CHILD

Some children discover at an early age what they want to do with their

94

lives. Like heat-seeking missiles, they lock in on their target and never deviate from their course. Because they clearly define their objectives and pursue them relentlessly, these intensely goal-oriented children often attain remarkable success. From their ranks come Olympic gold-medalists, computer geniuses, violin virtuosos, brilliant scientists, ballerinas and acclaimed novelists. Although clearly endowed with special abilities, the success of these super achievers is attributable only in part to natural talent. Equally vital in the equation is their singleness of purpose and their extraordinarily high level of dedication.

Achieving children share four basic traits:

1. They select their targets.
2. They identify the challenges and barriers that stand between them and their objective.
3. They carefully examine and assess their options.
4. They do what needs to be done to get the job done.

To be goal-oriented, a child need not be a potential superstar. Indeed, many children with less than exceptional abilities are able to attain remarkable success because they learn how to utilize their talents to the fullest. The high school athlete who lacks superior natural talent may not become a starter on the baseball team, but he can usually make the squad if he is willing to work hard enough.

Although the smart child may not realize on a conscious level that goals provide his life with a sense of direction and purpose, he intuitively senses their connection with achievement. The child instinctively realizes that attaining his objectives will produce rewards that more than compensate for any sacrifices that might be required.

One of the primary characteristics of the goal-oriented child is a willingness to suspend immediate gratification to achieve his long-term objectives. For example, if faced with the choice of spending the ten dollar gift from his grandmother playing games at the video arcade or saving the money to purchase a similar software program for the family's computer, the child would probably sacrifice immediate pleasure for more extended pleasure. Recognizing the value of self-restraint, he knows that once he buys the program, he can play the game whenever he wants.

It matters little whether a child's goal is as mundane as obtaining a computer game or as lofty as gaining admission to a first-rate music conservatory. Both goals serve parallel functions: they stimulate the child's desire to work and achieve, and they provide him with an opportunity to test himself and to develop his resources. When a child discovers that he is able to attain his goals, he is on his way to developing self-confidence and self-esteem.

The goal-directed child knows where he is headed, and he is propelled by a powerful fuel. The fuel is called motivation, and the higher its octane, the more the child will achieve. Because the non-goal-directed child runs on low-octane fuel, his engine is unable to generate the same number of rpm.

Highly goal-oriented children are driven by intense desire. Martin, for example, participated in the grueling training program because he recognized that this was the price he had to pay to improve his skills and his chances of winning an athletic scholarship. Making the Stanford water polo team was far more important than playing with his friends or watching TV after school. His dedication and desire made a training regimen that would have been unbearable for many other children actually pleasurable.

Only a relatively small minority of children naturally orient toward long-term objectives. Most children need to be inspired before they define their goals. For example, an unmotivated high school student may be profoundly influenced by her biology teacher and may decide that she wants to become a biologist. She begins to devote more time to her studies, and especially to science. Her priorities shift. She voluntarily forgoes opportunities to spend time with her friends in order to do her homework. Getting an "A" on the next test and in the course becomes a primary focus in her life. As she attains her objectives, her self-confidence grows, and she carefully maps out a strategy for getting into a first-rate college and ultimately into a first-rate graduate school.

DETERMINING IF YOUR CHILD IS GOAL-ORIENTED

Most parents know whether or not their child is adequately goal-directed. The parents of the non-goal-oriented child, however, may not know why their child lacks a sense of purpose and direction. The following goals checklist is designed to help you identify the specific attitudes and behaviors that are responsible for your child's deficient goal-orientation. A similar checklist for children follows on page 98.

Checklist for Parent GOALS

Code: 0 = Never   1 = Rarely
      2 = Sometimes   3 = Often   4 = Always

My child defines specific objectives.   _____

My child's goals are realistic.   _____

My child takes the time to plan ahead.   _____

My child is able to establish priorities.   _____

My child is able to budget and manage time   _____
effectively.

My child can develop a workable plan for   _____
attaining his or her objectives.

My child establishes interim goals.   _____

My child is willing to suspend immediate   _____
gratification in order to attain his or her goals.

My child bounces back from setbacks.   _____

My child can handle frustration.   _____

My child persists despite encountering difficulty.   _____

My child likes challenges and likes to test   _____
himself or herself.

My child believes he or she can prevail.   _____

My child is proud of his or her   _____
accomplishments.

My child establishes a new goal once he or she   _____
attains a particular objective.

TOTAL   _____

Interpreting the Checklist

If your child has scored *above* 45 on the checklist, he or she is probably
adequately goal-directed and strategic. Children scoring *below* 45 would
benefit from the activities and exercises that follow.

Your Child's Goals Checklist

It would be advisable for you to compare your perceptions about your child's goal-orientation with those of your child. To do so, ask your child to complete the following Goals Checklist.

This checklist is primarily intended for children seventh grade and above. Please note that your child may need to have some statements explained. Be sure to emphasize that the purpose of the checklist is to permit both of you to examine attitudes about goals and methods for achieving goals, and re-emphasize that the reason for totaling the score is to permit a comparison with a follow-up checklist that will be completed at the end of the book.

The statements on the checklist are designed to avoid a lot of "I don't know . . ." answers. This type of evasive response is typically produced under the following conditions:

1. The child feels he is being "grilled" by his parents.
2. The child is asked to consider issues to which he has previously given very little conscious thought.
3. The child is being asked questions that are too general or abstract.

If you use your child's responses to the statements as a springboard for discussion, do not react critically. Should your child state that he is rarely willing to work for something when he is frustrated, you might respond, "What I think you are saying is that when you run into a problem, you become discouraged and want to give up. Would you give me a specific example of something that has made you feel like giving up?" Ideally, the discussion will evolve from this point. By reacting in this way, you are creating an opportunity for your child to examine feelings and attitudes in a non-threatening context.

Activities and dialogues specifically designed to develop your child's goal-setting skills can be found later in the chapter.

Checklist for Child
GOALS

Code: 0 = Never   1 = Rarely
      2 = Sometimes   3 = Often   4 = Always

I have goals that I want to achieve.   _____

My goals are realistic. _____

I establish specific objectives. For example, I know _____
what grade I would like to get in each of my
courses.

I feel that I have the ability to get what I want. _____

I figure out a plan for reaching my long-term goals. _____

When I have a project or assignment to do, I _____
decide what steps I must go through in order to
reach my goal.

I am able to schedule my time so that I can get my _____
work done.

I am able to establish priorities (what's most _____
important).

I am patient as I work toward reaching my goals. _____

I enjoy learning new skills. _____

I enjoy improving my skills. _____

I am willing to continue working hard even if I _____
have a problem or a setback.

I am willing to continue working hard even if I _____
become frustrated or upset.

I like challenges. _____

I feel good when I overcome a challenge or a _____
problem.

When I achieve my goal, I feel proud. _____

I like to set a new goal for myself after I achieve a _____
particular goal.

TOTAL _____

Helping Your Child Interpret The Checklist

You might explain the "results" of the checklist in this way:

Possibility 1: Your score is _above 45,_ and you have a good system for
establishing and achieving goals. Although we don't need to

99

spend a lot of time doing the exercises in this chapter on goals, we could do them just for fun. You decide.

Possibility 2: Your score is *below 45,* and this suggests that you need some help in the area of establishing goals and planning ahead. Let's work together on some of the goal-setting activities in this chapter so that you can improve your skills in this area.

SMART AND PRACTICAL

Because the smart child is practical, he recognizes that it may be necessary sometimes to establish goals even in those areas in which he is not particularly interested or talented. For example, he may not be enthused about learning Spanish or chemistry, but because he thinks smart, he realizes that his overall grade-point average will be a primary factor in determining whether or not he is accepted at the college of his choice. To improve his chances, he will establish minimum target grades in all of his subjects. He will define specific short-term objectives such as a minimum of B + on all vocabulary quizzes, a minimum of B on all weekly tests, and a minimum of B- on all midterms and finals. If he wants to go to a prestigious college or university, he will have to target even higher grades in his courses.

Most parents are aware of the academic and vocational implications of deficient motivation. They know that their child will one day enter a world that is highly competitive, and they realize that without adequate skills and motivation, their child will be at a serious disadvantage. Ironically, this concern and awareness of the potential consequences can actually work at cross-purposes with correcting the situation, especially if the parents fall into the trap of continually expressing their disappointment and dissatisfaction.

Waiting for a child to develop a sense of direction can be an excruciating experience for parents who are themselves highly goal-oriented. The frustration can be particularly intense when parents are convinced that their child is wasting precious talents. Perceiving their child as drifting aimlessly and irresponsibly through school and life, these parents may fear with some justification that he will never "get his act together."

Most parents recognize that goals, desire, success, self-esteem, and self-confidence are inter-related. The cycle can be represented graphically:

100

ACHIEVEMENT LOOP

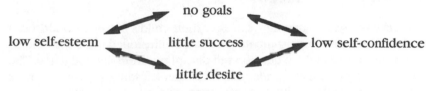

goals

self-esteem   success   self-confidence

desire

You will note that the arrows in the cycle point in both directions. This underscores the fact that the loop can turn in either direction and that any component in the cycle can be the catalyst that activates the loop.

The antithesis of this loop can also be represented graphically.

NON-ACHIEVEMENT LOOP

no goals

low self-esteem   little success   low self-confidence

little desire

If you conclude that your child is locked into a non-achievement loop, it is understandable that you would feel concern and a strong desire to intervene. However justifiable your concern and desire to intervene, the most appropriate response may be restraint. This is especially true in the case of parents who tend to express concern in the form of disapproval. Continual criticism produces discouragement, resentment and resistance and rarely changes a child's behavior.

The child who concludes that he is a disappointment to his parents is a prime candidate for becoming either hostile and resentful or anxious and insecure. If he becomes convinced that he can never meet his parents' expectations, he may begin to sabotage himself to "get back at them." The child who perceives himself as oppressed and incapable of satisfying his parents is a prime candidate for shutting-down or self-destructing.

If you are concerned about your child's lack of goal-orientation and motivation, you have other options besides continually expressing dissatisfaction. The first step is to remind yourself that your primary objective is to effect changes in your child's behavior and attitudes. You can do this far more effectively by taking a positive rather than a negative approach. By showing your child *how* to establish personal goals and *how* to focus his energy on attaining these goals, you can avoid the resentment and resistance that typically result when a child feels he is being attacked. (Methods for showing children how to establish goals and priorities are presented later in this chapter.)

Urging your child to establish objectives that are consistent with his personality, abilities and desires is vital. Equally vital is developing an effective communication "delivery system" that elicits cooperation and active participation.

The thrill of establishing and achieving goals can become addictive. With a carefully developed strategy, you can lead your child to appreciate that the habit of establishing goals can make life easier. In time, this habit will become "second nature."

AVOIDING QUICKSAND

Parents who believe that they can alter their child's behavior or attitudes with lectures or admonishments are soon disillusioned. Admonishments rarely motivate a child to develop self-discipline, effort and diligence. The lecturing parent usually finds himself or herself enmeshed in a power struggle. Two predictable response patterns typically emerge:

Symptoms

lecture → passive resistance
{
procrastination,
irresponsibility
forgetfulness
blaming
non-cooperation
}

lecture → rebellion
{
rule-breaking
lying
cheating
delinquency
drugs
}

Certain statements are red flags that signal a child that a lecture or sermon is forthcoming. These include:

★ "You should be more responsible."

102

★ "You need to have more self-discipline."
★ "You should be more organized."
★ "You need to pay more attention to details."
★ "You need more follow-through."
★ "You must stop putting things off to the last minute."
★ "You need to establish priorities."
★ "You should establish specific goals for yourself."

As soon as a child hears this type of admonishment, he will typically put up a defensive wall. Before statements such as "be more organized" or "establish your priorities" can have impact, the concepts must be made relevant, concrete and meaningful to a child. This means using examples to illustrate what the concepts mean and showing the child *how* to become organized and *how* to prioritize.

By creating opportunities for your child to experience and comprehend the benefits of establishing goals and priorities, you can significantly reduce a child's natural tendency to resist any proposal that involves change. Three practical steps can facilitate this process:

1. *Demonstrate how goals and priorities can actually make your child's life easier.* Use concrete examples, but don't lecture or give sermons. Share experiences in your own life in which goals helped you get the job done (e.g., "Do you remember last fall when we decided to go to the mountains on a ski trip and we had to decide what to bring with us? There were five of us and the car could only hold so much stuff. Mom and I and you kids had to make up a list . . .").

2. *Demonstrate how your child can establish goals and priorities in his own life.* Again, use concrete examples (e.g., "I'd like to do an experiment. Tell me the grades you would like to aim for in each subject on your next report card. We'll write these target grades down. The grades will be your goals in your courses, and we'll see when the report card comes how close you came to achieving your goals").

3. *Structure ample opportunity for practicing and examining goal-directed behavior* (e.g., "Let's set up a system with which you can record your grades on quizzes, tests and reports. In this way, you can keep track of your performance and see if you are moving toward your target grade in the course"). The spirit of these sessions should be cooperative, supportive, non-threatening and non-critical. (Yes, being non-critical when you're distressed is a challenge!) Sometimes, of

103

course, "coming down hard" and getting angry *is* appropriate. You must rely on your judgment and intuition.

Parents who do not develop a carefully conceived strategy in advance should not be surprised if their child resists relinquishing his non-goal-directed behavior. Methods for applying and practicing these steps are presented later in this chapter.

ESTABLISHING LONG-TERM GOALS

A child does not need to know at the age of 8—or even at the age of 18—what he wants to do with the rest of his life. Many career decisions made during early childhood are influenced by soon-forgotten fantasies. The 10-year-old child who proclaims that she wants to be a professional stuntwoman may have just seen an award ceremony on TV honoring stuntmen and women. Although her goal is probably temporary, it nevertheless serves an important function. The child is beginning to appreciate the value of focusing her energies on an objective.

Children who make career decisions at an early age and who remain committed to them throughout their lives usually have a special talent in a particular area. Such children naturally gravitate toward activities that capitalize upon this talent. The acknowledgment and affirmation they receive for their achievements create an emotional support system that sustains them throughout any trials and tribulations they might experience.

The goal-directed child stands out from the rest. A 9-year-old, for example, may be convinced that he will one day quarterback a professional football team. Once committed to his goal, he focuses his energies on attaining his objective. Continually testing his limits, he strains to get the most out of himself. If he is successful in high school and college, his motivation will increase, his self-confidence and self-esteem will grow and his commitment will solidify.

Goals encourage the development of *egoism*. This egoism is a reflection of the child's positive sense of himself and his confidence that he can make positive things happen in his life. Although sometimes confused with *egotism*, egoism is quite distinct from the arrogance and self-centeredness of the egotist. Without egoism, bridges would never be built, books would never be written, statues would never be sculpted and vaccines would never be discovered.

ESTABLISHING PRIORITIES

The goal-oriented child is also priority-oriented. At an early age, he realizes that life's possibilities are infinite and that the time required to avail oneself of these possibilities is, in contrast, quite limited. Although a smart 8-year old may not be consciously aware of the need to prioritize, he senses it intuitively and makes decisions accordingly.

Children cannot and should not be expected to organize their lives to the point where unstructured time and spontaneity are eliminated. Childhood is a precious time, and it would be a mistake to push children prematurely into a world of compelling responsibilities and obligations. Nevertheless, children do need to learn how to establish priorities, if for no other reason than to provide themselves with more free time to do the things they want to do. Although the responsibilities of a child are obviously more limited than those of an adult, a child must recognize that he does have responsibilities. Recognition of this fact of life is central to the development of character.

Defining specific, realistic responsibilities for your child (and ideally allowing your child to participate in the process of selecting his responsibilities) is a vital parenting function. By orienting your child toward responsibilities, you are orienting him toward establishing priorities. A child must be taught that doing his homework takes precedence over watching TV.

Even young children should have family responsibilities. For example, a 5-year-old might be assigned (or may choose) as one of his chores to set or clean off the dinner table. An 8-year-old might be given the job of feeding the dog. To avoid resistance, a list of family chores could be drawn up. The child would then be able to choose one or more from the list. The parents should also include in this list chores that clearly belong to them (e.g., supermarket shopping or paying bills). Once a job is chosen, it belongs to the child for an agreed-upon period of time. Later, chores might be traded among children in the family. The child's parents must clearly express that they expect the job to take priority over playing or TV and that they expect the job to be done by an agreed-upon time each day. They must also clearly communicate that they will not accept excuses. If the child can figure out how to get his chores done quickly and efficiently (by means of smart thinking), he will then have extra time to play, read, study, or watch TV.

Being able to establish priorities is an essential survival skill. Children who learn how to use their time effectively and who discover how to rank their responsibilities and objectives in order of importance or urgency have acquired an important resource that they will be able to use to advantage throughout their lives. (See Chapter 5.)

There are several possible explanations for why a child might fail to appreciate that studying for a history midterm or writing a book report is more important than going to the park and playing baseball with some friends:

1. A child may not have developed a clear sense of his obligations and responsibilities regarding his schoolwork.
2. A child may have been exposed to an environment that values educational effort and achievement.
3. A child may not have been adequately trained by his parents to develop self-control and may not be able to resist the temptation to satisfy his immediate desires.
4. A child may not have learned how to think strategically and may not consider the consequences of being poorly prepared for an exam or of failing to hand in a book report.

To achieve, children must be able to establish a hierarchy of what is important, and they must be able to define the steps that can get them where they want to go. The sooner they acquire strategic planning skills, they sooner they can begin to attain life's rewards.

The following dialogue models a strategy designed to help a young child appreciate the value of establishing priorities.

Model Dialogue #5
ESTABLISHING PRIORITIES
Children ages 7-12

Parent: How would you like to have a party?

Child: Really?

Parent: Dad and I will let you have a party on the condition that you plan it. How do you think you would go about doing this?

Child: I'd decide what kids I want to invite.

Parent: That's certainly important. Any other things that you would need to do?

Child: I'd have to decide what stuff to buy.

106

Parent:	For example?
Child:	Soft drinks. Potato chips. Ice cream. Maybe balloons and paper streamers. I'd also have to make sure we had good records for music.
Parent:	Where would you hold the party?
Child:	Maybe in the back yard if it's nice or in the den.
Parent:	Okay. Would you need to rearrange the den and maybe get more chairs for outside?
Child:	Yeah.
Parent:	What about shopping for everything? Since it's your party, we would want you to go with us to the store and help us.
Child:	Okay.
Parent:	You would have a lot of things to do. How would you remember everything?
Child	Make a list.
Parent:	Good. Are there things that you'd need to plan for first? For example, would you need to make up the list of kids you want to invite and send out invitations before you bought the soft drinks or potato chips?
Child:	Yeah.
Parent:	There is one very important detail that you forgot to plan. Can you think what it might be?
Child:	No.
Parent:	You haven't decided when you want to have the party!
Child:	Yeah! How about in 2 weeks?
Parent:	Okay. Why don't we say the party will be on Saturday, May 14.
Parent:	Let's make up the list of things you need to do, and let's put a number in front of each item. This number will tell you the order of importance and which things you need to do first. This is called establishing priorities—deciding what comes first and what comes next. First thing is to make up your list of kids. What should be second . . .

You will note that the parent in this dialogue introduces the concept of establishing priorities by using a situation that is relevant and non-threatening. Although she helps the child appreciate the value of establishing priorities as a means for attaining a desired objective, the mother is careful not to lecture. Once her daughter understands how to prioritize, the next step would be to show her how to establish the short-term objectives (e.g., purchase, fill out and mail the invitations, etc.) that will permit her to attain her long-term objective. The final step would be to set up a schedule (this step is examined in the next chapter).

ESTABLISHING SHORT-TERM GOALS

Some children intuitively figure out how to establish short-term goals. Others require guidance. A child who professes a desire to become a veterinarian may not realize that she has to get good grades in high school and college to be able to compete for admission to a veterinary school. She may have no idea how competitive the selection process is or how mentally challenging the academic demands of college and graduate school are.

Many children have little or no appreciation for the interim steps that are necessary for achieving a desired objective. These children characteristically take things as they come. In certain contexts this attitude is appropriate. Children should not be expected to plan meticulously everything they do. Goal-setting, prioritizing and scheduling, however, serve a vital function when there is lots to do and a limited amount of time to do it. The tenth-grader who has a book report due in 2 weeks had better schedule her time if she expects to read the book and get a good grade on the assignment.

Careful planning is a requisite to attaining goals. It is one thing for a child to say she wants to be a professional tennis player. It's quite another for her to realize what she has to do to achieve this objective. Helping her develop an awareness of the realities and required commitments reduces the risk of subsequent disappointment and disillusionment.

The following dialogues model strategies for presenting the issues of planning and establishing long-term and interim goals. Although it is preferable to begin encouraging children to establish goals when they are young, it is *never too late* to begin. If properly guided by their parents, teenagers can begin to develop a constructive goal-orientation. Their parents, however, must recognize that negative habits tend to become entrenched over time and that changing these habits requires patience and forbearance. The process must be taken one step at a time, and the

108

teenager must be allowed sufficient time to assimilate new thinking strategies and make behavioral changes.

Please note that the following dialogue addresses a specific event that may not be relevant to your family. Read through the dialogue anyway. It is intended to *illustrate* a process for establishing family goals in a cooperative, participatory manner. Once you have read the dialogue and examined the method, feel free to substitute a project that is more relevant to your family.

Model Dialogue #6
ESTABLISHING GOALS
Children ages 7-12

Parent:	Let's assume that the family agrees that we need a new floor in the kitchen because the old floor is showing signs of wear. We decide to replace it with a new tile floor. To save money, we decide to do the job ourselves, and everyone in the family agrees to help. How could we as a family do this job?
Child:	Buy the tile and then put it on the floor.
Parent:	Right. We need to get the material. What else?
Child:	I don't know.
Parent:	Well, let's list the things that need to be done. You've already told me that we need to buy the tile. Do you know how to lay tile?
Child:	No.
Parent:	Me neither. How do you think we could learn?
Child:	Buy a book.
Parent:	Right. We need to buy a book. Do you think that should be first on the list?
Child:	Yes.
Parent:	Okay. Do you think we need other materials beside the tile? Glue and tools?
Child:	Yeah.
Parent:	So we had better make a complete list of the supplies required. What next?

109

Child: I don't know.

Parent: Who's going to do the work? We have to rip out the old floor and then glue the new tile down. Some pieces will probably need to be cut to fit. We also have to decide on the design or pattern we want. Then we have to put in the grout—that's the stuff in between the tile. And finally, we have to clean off the excess grout around the edges. Lots of work, isn't it? How long do you think the job will take?

Child: Maybe a week.

Parent: Maybe. Perhaps even longer. What about eating? Will we be able to use the kitchen while the work is going on?

Child: I don't know. We could go out.

Parent: Too expensive.

Child: We have to eat, Dad.

Parent: Yeah. I've noticed you kids tend to get hungry and cranky when denied food. What could we do?

Child: We could do part of the kitchen each day.

Parent: Excellent idea! We really have to plan carefully, don't we, or we'll starve to death.

Child: Yeah!

Parent: Okay. What's our goal?

Child: To put in a new floor in the kitchen.

Parent: Who's going to do the work?

Child: We are.

Parent: Each person is going to have a job to do, right?

Child: Yeah.

Parent: We'll have to decide who does what. And then?

Child: We have to make up our list of stuff we need.

Parent: Right. And then?

Child: We have to plan so that we can still use the kitchen.

Parent: Right. What would happen if we didn't go through these steps?

Child:	We'd have a mess!
Parent:	Let's make up a chart. We'll write our long-term goal at the top: "Replace the Kitchen Floor with Tile." Let's call this our long-term goal because it will take us time to achieve it. Next we'll write down when we want to complete the job. This is our second long-term goal. Now we need to write down the short-term goals we've just discussed and a target date for each goal. Buy a how-to book by tomorrow. Read the book by next week. Buy the materials by the end of next week. Assign jobs to each family member. Plan each step so that we can still use the kitchen during the work. We also need to write down another important short-term goal: how much each family member agrees to work on the project. One person might be willing to work a minimum of 5 hours per week, and another might be willing to work a minimum of 10 hours per week. Each person could also indicate when he or she proposes to do the work. Later we can make up a more specific schedule. (See next page.) The "Goals Chart" might look like this:

GOALS CHART

	Target Date	Completion Date
Long-term Goal:		
Replace kitchen floor with ceramic tile.	OCT 15	_____
Short-term Goals:		
Read how-to book.	SEPT 2	_____
Buy materials.	SEPT 10	_____
Rip out linoleum.	SEPT 15	_____
Have one-half of the floor replaced.	SEPT 25	_____
Have second half of the floor replaced.	OCT 3	_____
Have finishing touches done.	OCT 5	_____
Have every member of the family work at least 5 hours per week on the project.	_____	_____

111

Assignments: (Fill in target dates.)
DAD
Buy book on laying tile. _____ _____
Buy plastic drop cloths. _____ _____

MOM
Pick out colors. _____ _____
Rearrange kitchen during work. _____ _____

CATHY, TRICIA, JEFF AND DAD
Buy tile and bring it home. _____ _____
Buy glue, grout and tools. _____ _____

EVERYONE
Lay tile. _____ _____
Remove grout. _____ _____

Parent: Did we forget anything?

Child: I don't think so.

Parent: I'm sure we'll think of other things as we go along. We can add them to the "Goals Chart." Why do you think it's important to have goals?

Child: So you know what to do and how to do it.

Parent: Excellent. Later, we will talk more about goals and scheduling time. We'll also figure out how you can use the same system in school.

The preceding dialogue models a method for encouraging a child to participate more willingly in a family project. By strategically involving the child in the planning stages, the parent is able to reduce the classic patterns of resistance that typically are triggered when a child feels coerced or oppressed. At the same time, the parent demonstrates in very concrete terms the value of establishing goals, determining responsibilities and creating a timetable. These are the "nuts and bolts" of developing organizational skills.

Sometimes it is possible to determine a timetable for a family project through consensus, as opposed to the parents arbitrarily assigning target dates. In the preceding dialogue, the parent defined the timetable somewhat autocratically. Parents must "read" each situation and decide whether a democratic or autocratic approach is advisable. The maturity level of the children must also be considered.

In the following dialogue, the concept of active participation in the process of establishing objectives is again modeled. This time, however, the parent is communicating with a teenager.

Model Dialogue #7
ESTABLISHING GOALS
Teenagers ages 13-17

Parent:	Mom and I are considering your request for a car. How do you think this should be handled?
Teenager:	What do you mean?
Parent:	Well, cars are expensive, and so is insurance. Are you expecting us to buy the car for you?
Teenager:	I don't have enough money.
Parent:	True. Do you think you should have to pay for the car?
Teenager:	No.
Parent:	Do you think you should contribute?
Teenager:	I guess.
Parent:	Mom and I feel very strongly that you should pay for at least half of the car and half of the insurance. How do you think you could accomplish this?
Teenager:	I could get a job.
Parent:	That's makes sense. How would you go about getting a job?
Teenager:	I'd have to apply for one.
Parent:	What would the first step be?
Teenager:	Find out what jobs are available.
Parent:	How could you do that?
Teenager:	Ask friends if they know about any jobs. Also I could go into the local stores and ask them if they need someone.
Parent:	Those are both good ideas. I suppose you could also look in the local paper.
Teenager:	Yeah.
Parent:	So, to solve the problem about sharing the cost of the car and

113

the insurance, you propose to get a job. Your goal is to earn the necessary money. To do this, you have to establish an immediate goal: get a job. Do you have any other requirements?

Teenager: What do you mean?

Parent: For instance, how much money you want to make, how many hours you want to work each week, and when you want to work. Do you think determining these things is important?

Teenager: Yeah.

Parent: What do you think about putting the goals and conditions into some sort of system? We could make up a chart that lists your long-term, your medium-term, and your short-term goals. Let's see how we could set it up. It might look something like this.

LONG-TERM GOALS

1. Earn enough money to pay for one-half of car and one-half of insurance. Target date: October of next year.
2. Get a job now for the school year.

SHORT-TERM GOALS

1. Get a job that pays at least $4 an hour. Target date: October 2nd.
2. Work a minimum of 12 hours per week during school year.
3. Save at least $25 per week to use for car and insurance repayment.

MEDIUM-RANGE GOALS

1. Work at least 30 hours per week during summer.
2. Save $85 a week to use for car and insurance repayment.
3. Pay off 25 percent of money owed on car and insurance by July.

Parent: Does this sound reasonable?

Teenager: Yes.

Parent: Okay. You have your goals established. You have a strategy for looking for a job. What's left?

Teenager: Doing it.

Parent: Right! Let me know if I can be of any help. Later, we'll talk about how the goal-setting system might be used in school.

The preceding dialogue presents a communication strategy expressly designed to encourage active participation in the process of establishing goals. You will note that the parent does not say, "Young man, you need to begin paying your own way. You can't expect to be given everything you want. Why, when I was your age, I was already paying for my room and board." This approach is all but guaranteed to trigger a defensive reaction. Rather than lecture or preach, the parent _shows the teenager how_ to identify the problem and _how_ to establish short, medium, and long-term goals as a means of resolving the problem. With sufficient practice, the teenager can begin to make goal-setting an integral part of his life. Had he concluded that his parent was primarily intent on delivering a lecture, he would have felt resentment and would have probably resisted his parents' efforts.

EXERCISING PARENTAL SELF-RESTRAINT

Imposing unrealistic or inappropriate goals on a child can have dire consequences. The danger is especially high when parents attempt to impose their own goals on their child. The potentially disastrous effects of disregarding a child's needs and temperament are underscored in the following column published in the _San Francisco Chronicle_ (August 20, 1986).*

The Dangers of Playing for the Folks
by Chris Dufresne

A few weeks ago in Huntington Beach, an angry parent rushed out of the bleachers during a youth league baseball game and allegedly decked a 16-year-old umpire over a "blown" call.

Recently in El Centro, the final eight games of a Little League season were canceled after another so-called adult jumped out of the stands and threatened an umpire with a knife.

The ballplayers in question here were 8-year-olds. You hear stories like those and realize that nothing ever really changes, that too often the games of children are still played for adults. It was that way 20 years ago and probably 40 before that.

We all knew kids in Little League or Pop Warner football who kept one eye on the ball and one on the stands. We've heard stories of sons who played $20-a-homer with their dads. We all felt the aching tug in our

*©1986 Los Angeles Times. Reprinted by permission.

stomachs when the bases were loaded and we were at bat.

It can be serious business, being a kid, especially for the ones who don't want to be out there in the first place.

Whenever I hear stories about kids and parents and sports, I can't help but think of a boy named Harold.

Harold was one of my teammates on a midget Pop Warner team in north Orange County. We were eighth-graders.

I didn't know him well, but I do know that Harold had no business playing football.

I didn't know his parents and can't begin to question their motives. I can't tell you why or even if they pushed their son out of the car every day for practice. As an eighth-grader with glowing red hair and swizzle sticks for legs, I had my own problems.

What I remember most about Harold is the sight of him crying. He cried almost every day.

Harold was a bona fide clod. His uniform hung on him like an oversized suit. He made a clanking sound when he ran, shoulder pads flapping underneath his jersey. Harold's pants drooped in the seat and his thigh pads roamed around his upper legs, protecting everything but his thighs.

When we ran wind sprints, Harold cried. When we crawled on all fours up the dirt hill behind our practice field, Harold cried. When we had tackling drills, Harold cried even more.

We, of course, handled Harold with all the tact of eighth-graders. We knocked him around like a pinball. He was an easy target, and no matter how bad you were, you always looked better after tackling Harold.

When Harold cried, we laughed. With collective wit we reminded him daily that crying was for babies, not for ones so close to puberty.

That all changed one day.

There's a tackling drill in football in which two players lie flat on their backs about 10 yards apart. One player holds a ball. At the whistle, the players jump to their feet and run toward each other like two locomotives locked on the same track.

I had a good view when Harold and a guy named Jim took their places on the ground. I was next in line to tackle. Harold held the ball against his stomach. The whistle blew and Harold ran toward Jim.

Jim hit him hard, helmet to helmet. We all cheered.

Harold didn't. Of course, he cried. Our coach ordered Harold to his feet and told him a few laps would shake the cobwebs from his head.

Harold took two steps and dropped to the ground.

Our coach cradled Harold in his arms but he wouldn't move. His eyes were wide open but they refused to blink.

I had never seen anyone die before. We were ordered to run laps around the field for no other reason than to keep us from staring. We ran for what seemed like hours, watching as they finally carried Harold off the field to the hospital.

The next day, someone explained to us something about how a blood clot had formed in Harold's brain and that the blow to the head was fatal.

Jim wasn't there to hear it.

We gathered as a team and, for some reason, voted to continue the season. Some of our mothers begged us to quit, but the only one who did was Jim.

We went to the funeral and went on with our lives, but most of us will never forget what happened that day.

I hope I remember long enough to tell a son of mine. Recently, I drove past my old Little League field and watched as one minor leaguer took his position in right field. I wondered if he really wanted to be there.

Sometimes I'll think of Harold and wonder what might have become of him. He might have been a great lawyer or an accountant. Maybe a space scientist.

We all knew he couldn't play football. But then, he never said he could.

Parents are responsible for shaping their child's character and values, and they are responsible for providing a home environment that encourages the development of the child's potential abilities. These responsibilities notwithstanding, parents do not have the right to force their child to become someone he is not suited to become because this image conforms to their own fantasy. Those who, for their own psychological needs, attempt to coerce their child into accepting a life plan at odds with the child's temperament or aptitude are embarking on a perilous path. All boys do not belong on a football field, and all girls do not belong in ballet class!

An important distinction must be made between pushing a child unrelentingly to become a physician, an engineer or a football player and encouraging a child to define practical goals such as getting decent grades, going to college or learning a vocational skill. Every child must learn that a certain amount of energy and effort is required to get him from point A to point B and that this energy and effort must be intentionally generated and carefully focused. The responsibility for helping a child appreciate cause and effect, however, is not a license to coerce him to do something that is not consistent with his talents, desires or personality.

DEALING WITH RESISTANCE

Some children balk at establishing even modest goals. Before responding with frustration or anger to this resistance, parents must determine if their child's behavior is attributable to irresponsibility or to the fact that he does not feel confident about his ability to do the job. What may appear to be procrastination may actually be a manifestation of self-doubt. Under such conditions, extra parental help and support are essential.

Before an insecure child would be willing to establish a challenging goal, he must be convinced that he has a chance to achieve the goal. A child already lacking in self-confidence cannot reasonably be expected to expose himself voluntarily to certain or even probable failure. (The exception would be the child who is intent on sabotaging himself.) Establishing goals is risky business for a child with a poor achievement track record.

The keys to defusing an insecure child's fear of failure (or success!) is to help the child establish realistic goals and to establish a game plan that will permit him to attain these goals. Success and self-confidence are powerful antidotes for resistance.

USING GOALS TO SOLVE PROBLEMS

Goals serve other vital functions besides those of producing motivation and focusing a child's energy. Once established, goals become an important weapon in the child's problem-solving arsenal. The child who concludes that he didn't get the grades he wanted on his last report card and who then establishes specific target grades and focuses his energies on attaining those grades is on his way to resolving his problem.

Establishing the goal of improving one's grades, however, is only the first step. The next step is for the child to figure why he is not doing as well as he would like. The final step is to develop a specific strategy for improving his performance. It is during this analytical phase that the child may need assistance from his parents in figuring out the "why, what and how." The ultimate objective is to get the child to the point where he can determine for himself the source of his problem and can then establish goals that will permit him to resolve the problem.

Goal-setting can make the previously described DIBS System (Define the problem, Investigate the issues, Brainstorm a solution and Select an idea to try) even more powerful. Just as the process of introspection was grafted onto the Examination phase (see Chapter 3), so can goal-setting be grafted onto the Brainstorming phase. If properly handled, the brainstorming process should produce specific problem-solving goals. An application of this expanded DIBS System is found below.

The Expanded DIBS System
USING GOALS TO SOLVE PROBLEMS
Teenagers ages 13-17

Define Problem: You have told us you want to go to a private college when you graduate from high school. As you know, we have put away money for your education. But it will not be enough to cover all of your expenses at a private college. So we have a problem. We need to plan together about how we can obtain the necessary funds.

Define Issue: Let's look at the issues. The first issue is to determine how much money is needed.

Investigate Issue: Let's make a list of your probable expenses. We need to include tuition, travel, room and board, books . . .

Define Issue: What sources of funds can be tapped?

Investigate Issue: Let's make a list of potential sources. We'll include scholarships, part-time jobs while in school, summer jobs, loans . . .

Define Issue: How much should we provide and how much should you provide?

Investigate Issue: What specific expenses do you think you should handle? How could you find the funds?

Define Issue: What can we do if there isn't enough?

Investigate Issue: Would you be willing to attend a state university if we find that we can't meet the cost of a private college? Are there any other options

119

we can explore? What about a community college as a fallback position?

Brainstorm/
Establish Goals: Let's set some specific targets and goals that might help solve the financial problem.

1. How much money do you want to save for expenses before you go off to college?

   Goal: $_____

2. How much money do you want to earn per week while at college?

   Goal: $_____

3. When do you want to complete your research about possible scholarships?

   Date: _____

4. What grades do you want to aim for this year in order to improve your chances for a scholarship?

   Subject: _____   Grade: _____

   Subject: _____   Grade: _____

   Subject: _____   Grade: _____

   Subject: _____   Grade: _____

   Subject: _____   Grade: _____

   Subject: _____   Grade: _____

By incorporating goal-setting into the DIBS System, the parent in the preceding dialogue demonstrates for his child how a significant problem can be solved. With sufficient practice, a child or teenager can begin to internalize and use this expanded method to resolve a wide spectrum of social, family and academic problems.

PERIODIC REVIEW OF GOALS AND ACHIEVEMENTS

One of the primary objectives of the expanded DIBS System is to encourage your child to review his achievements and goals on a regular basis. The child who acquires the habit of periodically examining and re-evaluating his efforts and his objectives has a distinct advantage over the child who is not self-assessing. For example, a student who wants to enter an MBA program in graduate school must continually monitor and assess her performance. She must also periodically examine her academic program to make sure she is taking the right courses. If she concludes that she is not working efficiently or conscientiously enough, she will have to make some important adjustments. If she concludes (or is told by an adviser) that she is not taking the appropriate courses, she will obviously have to alter her program.

The student who develops the capacity to assess her performance and achievements objectively can make the smart decisions requisite to achieving her goal. This process of making expedient adjustments is central to smart thinking.

CHANGING DIRECTION

A child's goals are not chiseled in stone. Discarding goals and substituting others is an integral part of the maturation process. A child often changes directions for a very basic reason: the original goal no longer meets his needs or is no longer appropriate. For example, the child who proclaims that he wants to become a professional basketball player is facing discouraging statistical odds against achieving his objective. Perhaps only .001 percent of the young children who fantasize about becoming professional athletes will actually do so. At some point, the child must objectively assess his abilities and decide whether he has a realistic chance of attaining his goal. If he concludes that he doesn't and decides to abandon his goal, his decision must be considered both smart and reasonable.

Although your child will probably abandon many of the goals he declares during childhood, you must nevertheless be alert to chronic patterns of goal-abandonment. Scrutiny is particularly in order when a child establishes a habit of casually discarding commitments or of giving up whenever he encounters difficulty. This behavior pattern could create major problems for the child throughout his life.

There is no absolute litmus test for determining the appropriateness or inappropriateness of a child's decision to abandon a particular goal. The pivotal issue is whether or not the child's decision is reasonable. Making a rational decision to change directions is quite distinct from making rationalizations about giving up because an undertaking has become slightly challenging. The child who gives up each time he is frustrated or temporarily thwarted is signaling a tendency to sabotage himself, and his parents have legitimate cause for concern.

Chronic goal abandonment is distinct from the behavior of the child who wants to discontinue her piano lessons because she never really wanted to learn to play the piano and was forced by his parents to take lessons. This classic tug of war over the issue of piano lessons may involve another factor: the child may have been initially interested in piano but may have subsequently become disinterested. Under such conditions, little is gained by insisting that she continue her lessons. If, however, the child's desire to discontinue is part of a mosaic of discarded goals, her motives and behavior should be closely examined.

The typical pattern of chronic goal abandonment can be represented by the following "formula":

Goal

Initial Enthusiasm

Struggle

Complaints

Abandonment

The following dialogue models how parents might deal with goal abandonment. The dialogue is oriented toward younger children. The same approach might be used with teenagers, although the tone of the dialogue would obviously have to be upgraded.

Model Dialogue #8
EXAMINING THE ABANDONMENT OF GOALS
Children ages 7-12

Parent: I was surprised when you told me that you want to drop your karate class.

122

Child: It's no fun. I hate karate and I hate the instructor.

Parent: You are frustrated.

Child: I guess.

Parent: Perhaps you expected to make more progress.

Child: I wanted to get my next belt, but he won't let me.

Parent: I thought you had to win the belt in a match.

Child: Yeah. But he won't advance me to the next level so I can win it.

Parent: I assume you feel you've been working very hard.

Child: Yeah, I guess.

Parent: Do you think the instructor suspects that you're not working hard?

Child: I don't care. I don't like karate.

Parent: You want me to let you drop out?

Child: Yes.

Parent: What would you expect me to do if you announced that you didn't like reading anymore? Would you want me to take you out of school or ask your teacher not to make you read?

Child: No.

Parent: Do you think that if I let you out of everything that was difficult, I would be a good parent?

Child: I don't know.

Parent: Well, if I did let you quit everytime something became difficult for you, I think that I would be a horrible parent. I would be sending you a message that you could give up anything that was challenging or anything you didn't like. Is this true?

Child: I guess.

Parent: I think it would be unfair to insist that you stay in karate if you really don't like it. At the same time, I think it would be unfair if I allowed you to drop the program now. This is what I'm willing to consider. I want you to work very hard and earn your next belt. When you do, we'll discuss the matter again. If you still want to quit, you can do so. Should you decide to drop karate, I want you to do so as a winner who

123

	has succeeded in reaching a goal. Do you think this is fair?
Child:	Yes.
Parent:	Good. I'll expect you to give 100 percent and not complain. If there are any problems between you and the instructor, we will talk to him and see if we can work things out. Do we have a deal?
Child:	Yes.

Before discussing the issue with his son, the parent in the preceding dialogue had formulated a strategy. Although he recognized the danger of permitting his son to give up each time he encountered a setback or frustration, he also recognized that little would be gained by insisting that the boy continue his karate lessons indefinitely. He was prepared to allow the boy to abandon the lessons only after he completed the next segment successfully. By structuring the "deal" this way, the father established a minimum standard of performance and helped the child appreciate the value of perseverance.

ACQUIRING SELF-DISCIPLINE

Adults who have faced life's challenges know all too well that self-discipline is a requisite to achievement. Some children seem to inherit natural self-discipline. Others must be helped to acquire this characteristic.

To someone lacking in self-discipline, the control and dedication of the goal-oriented person may appear remarkable. The phenomenon, however, is deceptive. People with self-discipline know a secret that those without it do not know: *self-discipline is easy when you are doing what you want to be doing.*

The committed runner voluntarily gets up at 6 a.m. to run her daily 6 miles. The inspired writer voluntarily works late into the evening to edit her work. To someone who dislikes running or writing, such a regimen would require ultimate discipline. To the committed writer or runner, the regimen becomes a natural part of her life. The runner enjoys conditioning her body, and the writer enjoys the thrill of creating her novel. Both would be miserable if denied the opportunity to do what they enjoy doing. This does not mean, however, that the writer and the runner do not struggle periodically with themselves and with the demands of their chosen pursuits. What distinguishes them from the rest is that when they encounter an impediment, they persist, partially because they have self-discipline,

124

but primarily because they are committed to attaining their personal goals and enjoy what they are doing.

The starting point in the process of orienting your child toward acquiring self-discipline is to help him discover his talents and interests. The parents of an artistic child would recognize the value of enrolling her in an art class, and the parents of a child who has a natural facility for soccer would recognize the value of enrolling him in a quality soccer program.

Although self-discipline may be selective and manifest itself in only one area, it often spills over into other areas of a child's life. The athlete who wants to win a scholarship to a university probably recognizes that she also needs decent grades. She may devote most of her time to sports, but if she is astute, she will create sufficient time in her daily schedule for study so that she can win the athletic scholarship she covets.

Although developing self-discipline is clearly desirable, there is a potential danger if self-discipline is carried to the extreme. A highly disciplined, goal-fixated child may become so absorbed by his special area of interest that he fails to achieve emotional balance. His single-mindedness can exact a high price. For example, a child may spend hours practicing and playing football and neglect his schoolwork and social life. The parents of a fixated child have justification for concern and should explore their concerns with their child. The dialogue format and the DIBS System can be especially effective tools during this exploration. In the dialogue modeled below, the parent helps his child examine some attitudes and behaviors that could create serious academic problems.

Model Dialogue #9
REINFORCING THE VALUE
OF STRATEGIC PLANNING
Children ages 9-17

Parent: I'm very impressed with your dedication to basketball. You seem committed to becoming a first-rate player. Tell me what your long-term goals are.

Child: I want to play pro ball.

Parent: I think it's great that you have a long-term goal. What do you think you need to do to attain your goal?

Child: Become a great player.

Parent: And?

125

Child: Play really well in high school and get an athletic scholarship to a good university with a good coach.

Parent: Practicing 2 or 3 hours a day is part of the plan.

Child: That's the only way I can become better.

Parent: Tell me what you will need to do to achieve your goal of a scholarship to a first-rate university.

Child: Good recommendations from my high school coach and good statistics. I'll also need to play great when college scouts come to watch.

Parent: Is that all?

Child: I guess.

Parent: How about grades?

Child: If you are a super player, grades are not that important.

Parent: Let's assume that you want to go to a top-notch university with high academic standards. Like other high school seniors, you apply for a scholarship. Let's also assume that you are an excellent athlete and have a 2.1 grade-point average. Another excellent athlete who is applying for the same scholarship has a 3.1 average. Which student do you think will get the scholarship?

Child: I guess the one with the better grades, if we both play about the same.

Parent: I agree. You have shown how dedicated and hard-working you are when it comes to sports. Wouldn't it be a shame if, despite all your hard work, you didn't get the scholarship you wanted because your grades were not up to standard?

Child: Yeah.

Parent: Tell me what makes you a better basketball player than many of the other kids on the team.

Child: I have natural ability, and I work hard.

Parent: And you know what you want.

Child: Yeah!

Parent: Knowing what you want gives you a tremendous advantage over the other kids. I bet you're one of the most dedicated

126

kids on the team. Do you think some of your dedication needs to be expanded into other areas?

Child: I guess so.

Parent: Tell me again the quality that distinguishes you from most of the other kids on the team.

Child: I know that I want to be a professional basketball player.

Parent: Precisely. You have a very specific long-term goal. You also have short-term goals. For instance, I know that you have targets for yourself each week. You know how many points you would like to score in the next game and how many rebounds and assists you would like to make. You also have long-term goals: to be the captain of the squad in your senior year and to get a scholarship to a school like Notre Dame or Michigan. Your ability to establish goals sets you apart and makes you smart and powerful. How could you apply this natural smartness to schoolwork?

Child: I could set goals for myself.

Parent: Right. For example, what sort of short-term goals might you set?

Child: I could decide what grades I want to get on my exams.

Parent: Exactly. And what about long-term goals?

Child: I could decide what grades I want in each course at the end of the semester.

Parent: That makes a lot of sense to me. Maybe we could actually make up a sort of score card in which you state your objectives in each subject and then you check them off when you achieve them. If you don't achieve a particular objective, you would then do the same thing you do in basketball. You would analyze the problem and decide what extra work you need to do to achieve your goal. It might mean extra studying or even a tutor. The tutor would be like a coach. How does this strategy sound?

Child: Good.

Parent: Let's see if we can brainstorm a monitoring system and create an academic achievement score card.

127

Parent: Let's see if we can brainstorm a monitoring system and create an academic achievement score card.

Although the parent in the previous dialogue is careful not to dampen his son's enthusiasm for basketball and his intense goal-orientation, he recognizes the danger inherent in his son's singleness of purpose. Legitimately concerned about the teenager's obliviousness to the importance of academics, he strategically decides to capitalize upon the youngster's natural self-discipline and goal-orientation. Rather than lecture, preach or threaten, he helps his son identify the common denominator that connects athletic achievement and academic achievement. He also shows him how to rechannel some of his energy without having to detract from his enthusiasm for basketball and his dream of becoming a professional basketball player.

Goals do more than provide children with a sense of direction and focus. When youngsters develop the habit of establishing goals, they have acquired a powerful problem-solving resource. Once a child establishes a specific objective of correcting a particular problem, he can then create a practical strategy for attaining this goal. When he does attain the objective, he will discover that the problem has most likely disappeared.

To be able to use goals most effectively, children must learn how to budget their time. This is the subject of the next chapter.

Chapter 5
Time Management and Organizational Skills

SHE DID IT ALL

Sarah slammed the back door shut, pushed up the kickstand and guided her bike down the driveway. The Girl Scout meeting would start in 10 minutes, and Tricia's house was six blocks away. "I'll make it," Sarah assured herself. It would be tight, but the 11-year-old was rarely late. As she peddled along, Sarah thought about the things she had to do that evening after dinner. The meeting would be over at 5:45 and then home for dinner at 6:00. Once dinner was finished, she and her brother would clear the table and put the dishes in the dishwasher. Then she would head straight to her room to study. Twenty long division problems with decimals were due tomorrow, and she had to complete a book report that was due Thursday. The fifth-grader also had 25 new spelling words to begin learning. The quiz would be on Friday. Mom could drill her in the morning after breakfast, and she could read her history assignment on the school bus. Somehow, she would get it all done, if her brother didn't bug her. Peddling furiously, her long hair and brown sweater flowing behind her, Sarah winced as she thought about the little monster who was intent on making her life miserable. "If he so much as enters my room tonight, I'll slug him with a pillow." Mom and Dad kept assuring her that some day they would be good friends. Sarah had her doubts.

PROCRASTINATION

Like their adult counterparts, children can also find themselves in a desperate race with the clock. The child who has developed the habit of putting things off until the last moment usually loses this race.

Not all children, of course, have difficulty dealing with time. Children like Sarah generally have most situations under control. They are able to prevail over life's challenges because their *modus operandi* is to identify their objectives, establish their priorities, plan ahead, budget their time, organize their materials, and get the job done efficiently, effectively and on time. These work habits are distinctive characteristics of smart thinking.

In contrast to the Sarahs of the world, children with chronically poor time-management skills are usually oblivious to responsibilities, time constraints and deadlines. They live in a state of continual crisis, and their chronic procrastination produces stress and tension that usually negatively affects everyone in the family.

Procrastination is a classic response to the dilemma of having too many things to do and too little time to do them. It is a way of running away from reality. By putting off the project or the responsibility, a child is able to delude himself for a while that he doesn't really have a deadline or an obligation. When the delusion shatters, the flying shards create havoc.

The highly disorganized, procrastinating child has failed to learn—or has chosen to disregard—one of life's basic axioms: marginal preparation and planning produce marginal performance.

There are five common reasons why children procrastinate:

1. *Inadequate goal-orientation*
   A child who fails to establish objectives does not have much incentive for getting the job done. Even if such a child does establish a goal, he may not know how to plan the necessary interim steps. (See Chapter 4 for a discussion of goals.)
2. *Poor time-management skills*
   A child who is oblivious to cause and effect probably does not recognize that inefficient use of time and poor performance are directly linked.
3. *Disorganization*
   A child whose life is in chaos, whose possessions and study materials are strewn about the room, and whose desk looks like a disaster area most likely handles his academic and family responsibilities in an equally chaotic way. There are, of course, exceptions. Some children are able to compartmentalize their lives and are very organized in some areas while they are totally disorganized in others.
4. *Disinterest*
   A child may not be interested in projects that are assigned and may put

off doing the task until the last moment.
5. *Resistance*
   The child who is angry at his parents may "punish" them by not doing what they want him to do. Some children transfer this resistance to all authority figures, including teachers, coaches and baby sitters.

The work of the child with poor time-management skills and poor organizational skills is typically inaccurate, submitted late, never completed or never started. Leaving his book report to the last minute, the procrastinating child usually discovers that he lacks sufficient time (and motivation) to edit the report and hands in an assignment replete with spelling and grammar mistakes. (This assumes, of course, that he even bothers to submit it!) It also is likely that when the same child takes his history exam, he will also discover that he has not learned information his teacher considers important. Being oblivious to cause and effect, he will fail to see the connection between his poor grades and his poor preparation.

Procrastinating, disorganized children are usually masters at making excuses. They often defend their procrastination with the following classic rationalizations:

★ The teacher didn't say it was due today.
★ The teacher is "unfair."
★ The work is boring or stupid.
★ "I don't like the teacher."
★ "I forgot . . ."
★ "I didn't understand the assignment."

The child who uses these excuses is trying to deny responsibility for his counterproductive behavior and to justify his poor performance. Perceptive parents and teachers recognize that these rationalizations are transparent attempts to camouflage self-defeating habits. Although these defense mechanisms may be unconscious, they nevertheless serve an important pragmatic function: they permit the child to avoid having to confront his habits.

FAMILY INFLUENCES

The behavior of the child with chronically poor time-management skills invariably triggers family tension and disharmony. The most logical explanation for the behavior is that the child has not internalized a value

131

system that stresses responsibility. Such an explanation strongly suggests that the procrastinating child disregards the consequences of his irresponsibility because his parents have failed to define clearly their guidelines, standards and expectations. Although in certain cases, this explanation is accurate, it does not explain the conduct of all procrastinating children.

Some procrastinating children have actually been exposed to a firm and consistently applied value system that emphasizes responsibility and time-management. For complex reasons, these children have chosen to rebel against the system. In extreme cases, the behavior may indicate underlying anger and psychological turmoil, and family or individual counseling is advisable.

Excessive parental or societal pressure can also cause a child to reject his family's position on such issues as punctuality and responsibility. This pressure may be real or imagined. A child, for instance, may feel that his parents expect him to become someone he does not want to become or is incapable of becoming. Rejecting the family's values may be the most accessible means for the child to express his resentment and defeat his parents' intentions. This behavior often occurs when a child feels he is being compared to a brother or sister who are more able to fulfill the parent's expectations.

Sometimes children reject their parents' value system because they perceive the family values to be hypocritical. The child who hears his parents talk about being punctual and then sees them being non-punctual is going to become confused. He may procrastinate because he sees his parents modeling this behavior, despite their protestations to the contrary.

Children may also reject their parents' values because they have been strongly influenced by exposure to another value system. An extreme example of this phenomenon was the well-publicized case of a 13-year-old girl who attended an anti-drug lecture sponsored by her church and then reported her parents to the police because they were using drugs. In a less extreme case, a child may choose to procrastinate because he is influenced by a peer group that also procrastinates. Putting things off may be considered "cool."

The child who hasn't assimilated the family's position on such issues as responsibility, effort and punctuality cannot reasonably be expected to be responsible, diligent and punctual. Ironically, some children exposed to home environments in which their parents are irresponsible actually compensate by becoming highly responsible.

Children can be positively or negatively influenced by their environment. A child's acceptance or rejection of his family's position on key value issues often hinges on how his parents present and model their position. Children who are helped to understand their parents' rationale for a particular standard of behavior and who are properly guided and supported are usually less resistant to assimilating that standard of behavior.

It is not uncommon for children to go through periods of minor rebellion. Persistent, open rebellion on such issues as organization, establishing goals, and managing time, however, is a yellow warning flag indicating that the family needs to examine and improve its communication system. If the situation persists, professional counseling may be necessary. The sooner this counseling begins, the less danger there is of permanent alienation.

THE INEFFICIENT USE OF TIME

The effects of disorganization and poor time management can spread like ripples on a pond. If the pebble hitting the pond is large enough, the entire surface of the water will be disturbed.

Substandard performance is one of the major sources of repeated emotionally charged encounters between parents and children. These encounters are often quite predictable. The child functions counterproductively, and his parents respond in a scripted way that typically involves anger, recriminations and punishment. Unfortunately, this melodrama rarely resolves the underlying problem. The net result is usually a showdown, hurt feelings and resentment.

In their desperation, the parents of a procrastinating child may feel they have no alternative other than punishment to eliminate their child's self-defeating behavior. Although this traditional negative reinforcement technique sometimes works, it often does not. In time, children habituate themselves to the punishment cycle, and the negative reinforcement becomes a desired payoff. This phenomenon is especially prevalent in the case of a child who feels unworthy of success and who unconsciously structures failures for himself. Procrastination may simply be one of his means for structuring failure.

The parents of a procrastinating child may fall into the trap of creating a symbiotic relationship with their child that involves a pattern of nagging and criticizing followed by a dramatic and predictable "rescue." Despite their professed upset with their child's behavior, rescuing parents invariably help their child when he gets in a bind. Because he knows he will ultimately be saved, the child never develops his own problem-solving resources. In many cases, parents actually end up doing their child's work for him. Parents who are manipulated into creating this type of dependency, or parents whose own psychological needs consciously or

133

unconsciously cause them to structure the dependency, are sending a clear message: Mommy and Daddy will always be there to save you when you have a problem. The child on the receiving end of this message is being set up to remain irresponsible and dependent throughout his life. Once he becomes addicted to his parents' constant attention and excessive nurturing, being rescued can actually become a major source of recreation. Such a child has no incentive to grow up.

Teachers of procrastinating children can also be drawn into a child's "helplessness drama." They may react to the child's dependency by becoming resigned and by simply "writing the child off" as hopeless. Some teachers may try to modify the child's counterproductive behavior with poor grades or punishments. Others may be willing to spend extra time helping the child learn how to organize, manage and plan his academic work more effectively. The reality of 30 to 40 students in a class, however, often prevents this type of individualized monitoring and support, especially at the junior and senior high school level.

The procrastinating child is enmeshed in a highly predictable behavior/response cycle:

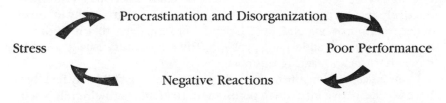

The reward for the child locked in such a loop is predetermined. His behavior allows him to be the center of attention and to manipulate and control his parents, teachers and peers. He can count on his behavior triggering a negative reaction. Although logic suggests that a child would not want a negative payoff, logic and emotions are not always congruent. If the child becomes addicted to negative attention, he can begin to crave the reaction he elicits by simply pressing certain "buttons." Having such power can appeal to a child who might otherwise feel powerless.

The child entangled in a procrastination/disorganization cycle is invariably unhappy and lacking in self-esteem. The negative responses he elicits reinforce his negative feelings about himself. Before long, marginal work and irresponsibility become the cornerstones of his identity.

A pattern of procrastination can have serious self-concept implications. Continual negative feedback in the form of poor grades, reprimands and punishment must damage a child's self-esteem and self-confidence. Once the child resigns himself to being hopelessly disorganized and inept, he can become overwhelmed by a sense of futility and impotence. Convinced of his incompetence, he will align his behavior and performance with this self-perception. This phenomenon can be seen in the case of the child who thinks he is "dumb" and who then reinforces this impression by intentionally acting dumb. Once a child's counterproductive cycle becomes permanently imprinted on his personality, it can influence his attitudes and behaviors for the rest of his life.

THE EFFICIENT USE OF TIME

The response system of the time-efficient child is very different from the one described above. The loop describing this child can also be represented graphically.

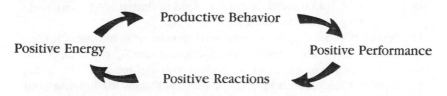

Children whose behavior conforms to this cycle feel good about themselves. They want to achieve, and they act in a way that improves their chances of achieving. As they experience more and more success, their self-esteem and self-confidence soar.

The time-efficient child also craves payoffs for his behavior, but unlike his disorganized, procrastinating counterpart, he seeks positive payoffs. Because he is committed to attaining his objectives and seeks his parents' and teachers' affirmation and acknowledgment, he does what is required to attain these rewards. In the process, he creates the identity of an achiever for himself.

The smart child recognizes that if he is to function efficiently and productively, he must deal effectively with the clock. Consequently, he plans ahead. He allows sufficient time to do the required research for his science report, and he budgets the necessary time for writing, editing and proofreading.

The plight of children who lack time-management skills is not hopeless. _With proper guidance, these children can be taught to use time effectively._

INTERVENTION

Poor work habits that have become enmeshed in a child's self-concept are particularly difficult to break. For this reason, early intervention is preferable. The sooner the intervention begins, the better.

Reorienting a child with poor time-management skills can pose a major challenge. Parents who frontally assault their child with their concerns and insist that there be an immediate change in attitude and behavior increase the potential for resistance. When parents are impatient and expect an instant transformation, they are generally setting themselves up for disappointment. Kids who feel pressured and oppressed can always figure out ways to thwart their parents' wishes if they are intent on doing so. The smart way to avoid this reaction is to convince the child of the value of the new behavior and to create a context of cooperation. Parents who strategically guide their child toward an appreciation of time-management skills significantly reduce the potential for resistance.

The first step in the behavior reorientation process is to pinpoint your child's time-management deficits. The following checklist can help you identify these deficiencies. Once identified, you can examine the issues systematically with your child. Methods and activities for helping your child internalize a more efficient system are presented after the checklist.

Checklist for Parent
TIME MANAGEMENT

Code: 0 = Never   1 = Rarely
    2 = Sometimes 3 = Often   4 = Always

My child leaves projects and assignments to the   _____
last minute.

My child doesn't seem to care about getting   _____
things done on time.

My child does not have a schedule.   _____

My child hands in material that is inaccurate and   _____
sloppy.

My child often hands in assignments that are   _____
incomplete.

My child does not hand in assignments.   _____

136

My child has difficulty estimating accurately how   _____
much time a project will require.

My child lacks planning skills.   _____

My child is often under stress caused by poor   _____
time-management.

My child does not consider the time required to   _____
perform the steps necessary for achieving an
objective.

My child schedules too many things to do at one   _____
time.

My child does not have leave enough time for   _____
reviewing and proofing his assignments.

My child is late for appointments.   _____

My child's time-management behaviors create   _____
stress in the family.

TOTAL   _____

Interpreting the Checklist

If your child's scored _above 24_ on the preceding checklist, he is having difficulty in the area of time management. If you are to help him become more time-efficient, you must show him how to use time effectively. Techniques for doing so are presented below. But first, it would be a good idea to have your child complete the following checklist.

Checklist for Child
TIME MANAGEMENT

Code: 0 = Never   1 = Rarely
      2 = Sometimes   3 – Often   4 = Always

I leave my projects and assignments to the last   _____
minute.

The work I hand in has errors.   _____

I do not hand in assignments on time.   _____

My work is sloppy.   _____

137

I get upset because I don't have enough time. _____

My work is incomplete. _____

My work is handed in late. _____

I have difficulty planning how much time I need _____
to complete a project.

I schedule too many things to do at one time. _____

I do not leave enough time to check over my _____
work.

I am late for school, appointments or meetings. _____

I don't use a schedule. _____

TOTAL _____

Helping Your Child Interpret the Checklist

It is important to help your child interpret his or her responses. You might want to use the following explanation: "If you scored above 23 on the checklist, it suggests that you could benefit from some work on learning how to use time more effectively. I'd like to do some activities with you. These activities should sharpen your skills in this area. Later you will fill out a similar checklist so that you can see how much progress you have made."

DEVELOPING TIME-MANAGEMENT SKILLS

Most children are willing to learn new skills if they are convinced that the skills can make their lives easier and more enjoyable. Conversely, most children resist learning new skills if they are convinced the learning process will be boring, painful or worthless. Children tend to reject parental wisdom when they are frontally assaulted, patronized or treated in a derogatory way.

Examples of statements almost certain to be rejected include:

★ "If you used your time more effectively, you could get your work done without having to go through a crisis every evening."
★ "If you stopped spinning your wheels and started to concentrate, you would remember more."
★ "If you didn't leave things to the last minute, you'd get them done on time."

138

★   "If you were more organized, you could save hours each day."

Wise parents avoid making statements such as these. They realize that a negative approach usually triggers a negative reaction. Rather than admonish, they attempt to involve their child actively in the process of making behavioral changes. Wise teachers come to the same realization. The teacher who is positive and who encourages active learning invariably achieves far better results than the teacher who is negative and who encourages, or permits, passive learning.

These basic teaching principles also apply at home. By involving your child in the process of learning and applying time-management skills, you significantly improve the chances that he will master and use these skills.

In the dialogue below, a mother examines the issue of budgeting time with her child and models an approach designed to reduce reactionary behavior.

Model Dialogue #10
MANAGING TIME
Children ages 7-12

Parent: Dad and I seem to be spending a lot of time getting on your case about getting your homework done. Is the stress as upsetting to you as it is to us?

Child: I guess.

Parent: Tell me why you think we're hassling you.

Child: 'Cause I put things off to the last minute.

Parent: I'm curious to know if there's a reason for this.

Child: I'd rather do other things. When I get home from school, I want to play with my friends, but you won't let me. You're always reminding me that I have homework to do. And then Dad gets home and he gets on my case, too.

Parent: When I hassle you about doing your homework, do you actually have homework to do?

Child: Yeah. Sometimes.

Parent: Do you see any solution to this problem?

Child: I suppose I could do my homework without having to be reminded.

139

Parent:	But you'd rather be out playing.
Child:	Yeah.
Parent:	Do you think it's possible to do your homework and still have time to play?
Child:	No.
Parent:	Well, let's see. If you were working real hard and were really concentrating on your homework, how much time would you need to do it?
Child:	One hour. Maybe an hour and 15 minutes.
Parent:	OK. Let's figure an hour and 15 minutes. I think that's a fair amount of time for a kid in fifth grade. Somedays you may need to spend a little more and somedays a little less. You get home from school at 3:30. What's the first thing you do when you get home.
Child:	Milk and cookies.
Parent:	OK. What would you like to do next?
Child:	Go out and play ball with my friends.
Parent:	That seems reasonable. How long do you want to play?
Child:	Till dinner.
Parent:	Remember, you do have to get in a minimum of one hour and 15 minutes of homework.
Child:	I could do it after dinner.
Parent:	You could. Dinner is usually over at 6:45. If you went right to work, and worked straight through, you would be done at 8:00. Bedtime is at 9:00. That would mean one hour for yourself after completing your homework. And it would be understood that there would be no TV until at least 8:00. Let's look at some other possibilities. What about playing from 3:30 to 5:15, and then spending at least one half hour on homework before dinner? It starts getting dark anyway at 5:00. This schedule would leave you only 45 minutes to do after dinner. Would that give you enough time to play?
Child:	Yeah.
Parent:	Okay. So you do have some choices about your schedule. When you study, you'll need some breaks to recharge your

140

batteries. Do you think it's reasonable to study for 20 minutes at a time and then take a 5-minute break?

Child: Yeah.

Parent: We could get a timer and set it to go off in 20 minutes. You would then study and really concentrate until the timer goes off. Agreed?

Child: Agreed.

Parent: Now the deal is that Mom and I won't hassle you if you keep to your study schedule. Agreed?

Child: Agreed.

Parent: I'm going to ask you to sign a written agreement about what we've decided. The contract will last for one month. Then if you want to make changes, we will take a look at the agreement and perhaps make revisions. We also need to decide about how much homework you'll need to do during the weekends and when you'll do it. One other thing. I'm willing to sweeten the deal. If you successfully keep to the agreement for one month, I'll get us some tickets to a football game. Sound good?

Child: Yeah!

Parent: Let's look at two schedules. One is a sample that shows how someone might budget his time. This is sort of a practice schedule. (Please note: This sample schedule reflects time agreements examined in the previous hypothetical discussion). The second schedule is blank, and we'll fill it in together. We'll plug in your study time and your play time and time for breaks, chores, dinner and getting dressed. Let's look at the sample schedule first. Then we'll decide not only how you want to use your time, but also how you can use your time most effectively.

141

SAMPLE WEEKLY SCHEDULE

Time	Mon.	Tue.	Wed.	Thur.	Fri.	Sat.	Sun.
3:30-5:15	Free	Free	Free	Free	Free	Free	Free
5:15-6:00	Study	Study	Study	Study	Study	Study	Study
6:00-6:30	Dinner	Dinner	Dinner	Dinner	Dinner	Dinner	Dinner
6:30-7:15	Study	Study	Study	Study	Study	Study	Study
7:15-9:00	Free	Free	Free	Free	Free	Free	Free
9:00-7:00 AM	Sleep	Sleep	Sleep	Sleep	Sleep	Sleep	Sleep

Parent: The beautiful thing about schedules is that they can be changed. To be effective, the schedule has to work for you. Now that we've looked at this sample schedule, let's fill in a schedule that you feel can make your life easier and provide you with free time for play, fun, reading or TV. OK?

Child: Yeah!

Parent: What do you think? Can you live with this schedule for a month?

Child: Yes.

Parent: After the month is up, we can make changes if you wish. You understand that I expect you to keep to the schedule with no arguments. You will finish playing with your friends at 5:15 and you'll be at your desk at 5:30 and do your work until dinner at 6:00. Agreed?

142

MY WEEKLY SCHEDULE

Time	Mon.	Tue.	Wed.	Thur.	Fri.	Sat.	Sun.
3:30-4:30							
4:30-5:30							
5:30-6:30							
6:30-7:30							
7:30-8:30							
8:30-9:00							
9:00							

Child:	Yes.
Parent:	And no TV until you finish your homework at 7:15.
Child:	Yes.
Parent:	And you also realize that some days you may need to work until 7:30 or 7:45 if you have a lot of homework.
Child:	OK. But what if I have only a little homework and I don't need an hour and 15 minutes to do it?
Parent:	You'll discuss it with us and we'll decide together if you can have more free time on that day. OK?
Child:	Yes.
Parent:	Good. We'll start the program tomorrow.

Parent:	You'll discuss it with us and we'll decide together if you can have more free time on that day. OK?
Child:	Yes.
Parent:	Good. We'll start the program tomorrow.

By intentionally involving her child in the process of determining his study schedule, the parent in the preceding dialogue reduces the risk of a showdown. Because her son actively participates in making key decisions about how he will use his time, he cannot assume the role of victim. The mother will have to do some monitoring, but her strategy relieves her of the responsibility of having to nag her son about doing his homework. Thus, she avoids being forced into the role of policewoman. Although she encourages her child's involvement in creating the ground rules, she establishes guidelines and clearly serves notice that she expects compliance with the agreed-upon terms.

The approach modeled above can be equally effective in communicating with teenagers. Parents who involve their child in the process of determining a mutually acceptable study schedule are thinking smart. This strategy should significantly reduce family tension. In dealing with teenagers, parents should be prepared to negotiate some of the issues, and when appropriate, to make some concessions for the purpose of family peace and harmony. Teenagers have a legitimate need to feel that they have some power over their own lives. This need signals their ongoing transition to adulthood. Although you may be convinced that doing 4 hours of homework each evening is realistic for a college-bound teenager, your child may not concur. Encourage experimentation and periodic assessments so that an appropriate study schedule can be determined. This assessment procedure will indicate whether or not the schedule needs to be altered or fine-tuned.

Your ultimate objective is to guide your child to a critical realization: effective time-management will allow him to exercise positive control over his life, and this control will provide him with more free time to do what he wants to do. Once your child realizes the power inherent in the efficient use of time, he will probably become a "convert." The next step is to help your child become better organized. This subject will be covered after the following supplemental activities.

Supplemental Activity
EFFICIENT USE OF TIME
Older Children and Teenagers ages 12-18

Parent: I'd like to examine a situation with you that I'm sure you've had to deal with many times in school.

Situation: You are assigned a term paper in history. It is due in 4 weeks. The paper is supposed to be eight to ten typed pages long and must include an introduction, a conclusion, footnotes and a bibliography. Does this type of assignment sound familiar? How much time do you estimate a project like this will require to be done well? OK. Let's look at the things that need to be done:

Let's see what happens when you rank the steps in order of priority and importance and determine the amount of time necessary for doing each step. [*Note:* If your child has not been properly taught in school how to do a research paper, you will need to explain the reason for the following steps and perhaps discuss how to perform them.]

HISTORY TERM PAPER SCHEDULE
Total Time Budgeted

*STEPS IN ORDER OF PRIORITY**	*ESTIMATED TIME REQUIRED*
_____ Take notes	_____
_____ Write conclusion	_____
_____ Do research	_____
_____ Proofread final copy	_____
_____ Write rough draft	_____
_____ Put notes on index cards	_____
_____ Organize your notes	_____
_____ Do bibliography	_____

*Put appropriate number of ranking

145

____	Put quotations on file cards	_____
____	Write introduction	_____
____	Correct rough draft	_____
____	Make outline	_____
____	Type paper	_____
____	Insert quotations	_____
____	Check footnotes for accuracy	_____
____	Select resource material that you will use for report (encyclopedia, text books, library books, etc.)	_____
	TOTAL	_____

Parent: Let's discuss your priorities and your time estimates. You've made decisions about the order of the steps and you've made estimates about how much time will be required to perform each step. Let's take a look at your reasons for these decisions. After we're examined the schedule, we'll put it aside. Later, when one of your teachers does assign a term paper, you can use it and see if the schedule was accurate.

Supplemental Acitvity
EFFICIENT USE OF TIME
Younger Children ages 7-12

Parent: I'm going to describe a situation and then you can put the steps in order.

Situation: You've decided that you want to give a party in 2 weeks. We have agreed to allow you to have the party, but have told you that you will have to do all the planning. Let's assume that you want to invite 25 kids. How long do you think it will take you to do all the planning? OK. Let's take a look at the steps, and you decide how much time you'll need to do each one.

146

PLANNING A PARTY
Total Time Budgeted

STEPS IN ORDER OF PRIORITY	ESTIMATED TIME REQUIRED
_____ Send invitations	_____
_____ Buy food	_____
_____ Hang decorations	_____
_____ Make up list of kids to invite	_____
_____ Buy drinks	_____
_____ Buy party decorations	_____
_____ Decorate family room	_____
_____ Heat up hot dogs	_____
_____ Select music	_____
_____ Plan games	_____
_____ Clean up after party	_____
TOTAL	_____

Parent: Good. You have decided on the order of the steps and estimated the time you need. Let's take a look at some of your reasons for placing certain steps ahead of others, and also let's take a look at why you decided to budget the amount of time you did for each step. Then we'll put your schedule away, and the next time you want to have a party, we'll take it out and use it. Then we'll see if your estimates are correct.

ENVIRONMENTAL CHAOS

Learning how to manage time efficiently is essential to thinking and acting smart. Learning how to organize available resources is equally essential.

The child whose life is in chaos spends too much time looking for things and too little time getting the job done. His wheel-spinning produces two predictable outcomes: it undermines his efforts, and it generates frustration and stress for the child and the entire family.

The smart child makes sure he has the necessary materials for getting the

147

job done, and he figures out how to organize these materials. If he is doing library research for a report, he writes important information on index cards that he can later shuffle, organize and reorganize. He meticulously records quotations and footnotes and stores his note cards in a file box. Because he is practical, he does everything in his power to make his life easier. This sense of order is one of the benchmarks of smart thinking.

The disorganized child's habits are at the other end of the efficiency spectrum. Because he has little or no structure in his life, he is in a continual state of chaos. His room is a mess. His notebook is a mess. His assignment organizer is a mess (assuming that he has an assignment organizer and bothers to write down his assignments). His schoolwork and personal life reflect the disorder with which he surrounds himself. On any given day, he might be found searching desperately for his math textbook or his baseball glove.

During the formative years, a child must be provided with external structure in the form of parentally imposed guidelines and rules. He needs to understand what he is and is not permitted to do. This structure creates a behavioral framework on which the child can build. It also protects the child from being confused and overwhelmed by decisions and choices he is not emotionally prepared to make. As he matures, the child will internalize this external structure. He will learn to distinguish right from wrong. Ideally, he will recognize that stealing, lying, cruelty and irresponsibility are wrong and that honesty, love, knowledge, responsibility and effort are right.

A child's internal structure manifests itself in the form of self-control. The child realizes that he must discipline himself to study and that he must resist the drugs offered to him at a party. Having accepted and assimilated his family's value system and its basic guidelines, he develops inhibitions. These inhibitions are both sign posts and boundary markers. They provide stability and order for a child in a world that might otherwise be unstable and disordered.

Children who have not internalized a sense of structure and organization during the early years of their development rarely work up to their potential. Ideally, the process of imposing external guidelines and performance standards should begin before the teenage years. Logic dictates that the longer a child has functioned counterproductively, the more difficult it will be to effect behavioral changes. However, even teenagers can begin to assimilate a sense of order and structure, assuming they are provided with proper guidance and assuming their parents are consistent, patient, supportive and fair.

If parents first begin to create external order relatively late in the child's

148

life (after age 7), they should be prepared for varying degrees of resistance. This is especially true when parents suddenly decide to impose a series of unrealistic and autocratic rules that overwhelm the child with conditions and consequences for misbehavior. If resistance and rebellion are to be minimized, the retraining process must proceed in stages. Lots of parental support and encouragement must be provided, and ample time must be allocated for a non-emotional examination of the issues, as well as for active involvement and practice.

Disorganization can quickly become an entrenched, hard-to-break habit. The disorganized child has not developed the inhibitions that would normally prevent him from functioning inefficiently. Changing his behavior patterns requires a strategy that incorporates clearly defined behavior guidelines, active participation, patience, effective teaching methods and good communication. Just as the child with poor time-management skills must be systematically taught how to use time efficiently, so must the disorganized child be systematically taught how to use materials efficiently.

The most effective way to help a child become better organized is to help him see the value of better organization. The associated skills must be introduced sequentially and in increments that the child can assimilate. Positive reinforcement in the form of praise and perhaps even rewards can significantly facilitate the process and can reduce potential resistance. The ultimate goal is for the child to become convinced that organization can make his life easier and provide him with more and better payoffs than disorganization.

Changing behavior is like breaking in a new baseball glove. You need to pound at it, oil it and shape it. Despite these efforts, it takes time before the glove fits right and feels comfortable. A child also requires time to mold new behaviors until they fit right and feel comfortable. The ultimate goal is to change the child's self-concept so that he perceives himself as being organized. This transformation in self-concept is vital to achieving a lasting transformation in behavior. The child who sees himself as being disorganized will create disorder in his life. Conversely, the child who sees himself as organized will create order. The most effective means for achieving this change in a child's self-concept is for parents to use a strategy that incorporates both introspection and behavior modification.

In the following dialogue, a parent examines the issue of disorganization with a 13-year-old who is unwilling to admit that he has a problem with organization.

Model Dialogue #11
DEVELOPING ORGANIZATIONAL SKILLS
Teenagers ages 13-17

Parent: It is my impression that you are having difficulty organizing your schoolwork? Am I correct in my impression?

Teenager: No.

Parent: Well, let me be more specific and share some feedback I've gotten from school and some personal observations. I have received several notes from your English teacher. She says that you are not getting your assignments in on time, that your work is incomplete and sloppy, and that you are often unprepared for class. I've observed that your study area is strewn with papers and that the materials you need to study are not organized into any sort of system. I've also seen you get frustrated and angry when you can't find something you need.

Teenager: I have my own system.

Parent: That's fine. But is the system working?

Teenager: Yes.

Parent: Your grades are in the C range. Do you feel that is the best you are capable of doing?

Teenager: No.

Parent: Do you have a strategy in mind for improving your grades?

Teenager: No.

Parent: One last question, and I'd like you to be frank with me. Do you want to improve your grades?

Teenager: Yes.

Parent: I'm going to propose a 1-month experiment that might help. I've checked with your teachers and counselor, and they tell me that your skills are fine. I also know that you are bright. So the reason you are doing marginally in school has nothing to do with a learning problem or lack of intelligence. I believe that the situation could improve dramatically if you developed some organizational skills. Give the proposed experiment an honest try. If I am wrong, and the experiment doesn't work, I will be happy to apologize. Will you give it a shot?

Teenager: I don't know yet until you tell me what the system is.

Parent: OK. Let's start out by making a list of the things you need in order to study efficiently. The basic things are obvious: a desk, a good lamp, a dictionary, pencils. There are perhaps other less obvious things.

For example, you will need a thesaurus when you are writing reports and essays. What other things can you think of? Let's write them down in order of importance. If there are things you need, I will give you the money to buy them. Now, tell me how you might set up your study area.

Teenager: I already have a desk in my room.

Parent: What could you do to organize your materials?

Teenager: What do you mean?

Parent: Do you have a filing system to keep your returned homework assignments, tests and reports?

Teenager: No.

Parent: Let's set one up. We'll need to buy you a small filing cabinet and file folders. What about putting a big master schedule on the wall facing your desk. You could write down the upcoming reports, exams and quizzes. How about a timer? You could set it for 30-minute study intervals.

Teenager: I don't know if I want to do all this stuff. It's going to take a lot of time.

Parent: I guarantee that once you get the system going, it will save you time. It's like learning to use a skate board. At first it's hard, and you fall a lot. You could probably walk faster. But once you are good at it, the skate board saves you a lot of time. It's the same when you first learn to type. It takes forever to get through one page. Later though, typing saves you lots of time. Let's design a personal organizational system that works for you. Use it for 1 month. I'll bet you will discover that you end up liking it. You'll have more free time, and your grades will improve. If you try the system, and it doesn't work, you can always go back to your old way of doing things. OK?

In the preceding dialogue, the parent is careful not to lecture her child about the value of organization. Rather, she shows her daughter how she can create more order in her life. She doesn't give any ultimatums (e.g. "If you don't straighten up your room and organize your schoolwork, Dad and I are going to ground you!") Nor does she resort to using guilt (e.g. "How could you be so inconsiderate of your father and me?") The mother strategically defuses any potential resistance by proposing a non-threatening experiment for a specific period of time. She then helps her daughter develop a practical system that would permit her to work more efficiently, and she gives her permission to reject the organizational system if she finds that it doesn't work.

By proposing an experiment and by giving her daughter some power, the parent wisely avoids a showdown. She also allows her daughter to decide if the system is helping. The parent, however, still has a "hold card." If the system does not prove as effective as desired, she could then propose that it be modified or fine-tuned rather than totally abandoned.

Offering to help her daughter set up a filing system allows the parent to demonstrate how returned tests, reports and notes can be categorized and filed. By suggesting that she make a list of things needed, she encourages her to develop and refine her prioritizing skills.[1]

In the following dialogue, a parent examines the issue of organizational skills with an 8-year-old.

Model Dialogue #12
DEVELOPING ORGANIZATIONAL SKILLS
Younger Children ages 7-12

Parent: When I walked through the garage last week, I saw that you had taken your bicycle apart. What's up?

Child: The chain came off, and when I tried to fix it, the gears wouldn't work.

Parent: It's been sitting there for a week, and Mom's upset because she can't pull her car in. Can you fix it?

Child: I can't get the gears to work.

Parent: I sense you're very frustrated.

[1] For more hands-on activities involving school-related organizational skills, see *Getting Smarter*.

Child:	Yeah. I want to use my bike.
Parent:	Would you like some help?
Child:	Yes!
Parent:	OK. How about if you put down some newspaper under the bike. This will help you find any parts that you might drop, and it will also keep grease off the floor. The next step is for me to find the instruction manual. I remember filing it in my office after we used it to put the bike together last Christmas. I'll go get it. In the meantime, you begin to lay out on the paper the tools you think we will need—screwdrivers, wrenches, etc.
Child:	I don't think we'll ever be able to fix this thing.
Parent:	If we go about it right, we will. Let's see if we have all the tools and the parts we need. We'll need the socket wrench kit and the Phillips screwdriver and the Allenhead wrenches. OK. Do we need anything else?
Child:	I don't think so.
Parent:	Were you planning on cleaning your chain also?
Child:	Yeah.
Parent:	What will we need to do it?
Child:	A bucket and water.
Parent:	We'll also need some detergent and some oil. OK let's look at the manual . . .

Once the bike is reassembled, the parent could review the steps and examine the rationale for progressing in an orderly, organized fashion. This should be done fairly quickly and in a non-preachy manner. The parent might then say: "What steps do you think you need to take whenever you begin this type of project?" The child and the parent could then create a basic operational system that could serve as a blueprint for all projects and assignments:

1. Define what needs to be done.
2. Set up the work area.
3. Make sure you have the necessary tools and parts.
4. Read through the instruction manual before beginning.
5. Ask for help if you can't figure something out.

153

At this point, the parent might help the child apply these organizational principles to other projects and assignments he can expect to confront. For example, the parent might say: "Let's assume you have a test coming up in math. How could you use these organizational methods to get the job done properly? Let's make a list of what you have to do, and what materials you'll need to get the job done."

The following activities are intended to help your child master and assimilate the organizational principles that have been presented in this chapter.

Supplemental Activity
REINFORCING ORGANIZATIONAL SKILLS
Children ages 7-12

Situation: Imagine that you are packing for a 5-day camping trip. Let's list the things you would want to take with you. When we're done listing them, we'll put them in order of importance. We'll also take a look at your reasons for including each item and your reasons for putting the item in a particular order of importance.

Supplemental Activity
REINFORCING ORGANIZATIONAL SKILLS
Teenagers ages 13-17

Situation: Imagine that you have an opportunity to join two expert sailors on a sailing trip from San Francisco to Hawaii. You are assigned the job of organizing a life-support kit that would be used in case of an emergency. Let's list what you would include in the kit. When you're done listing them, I'd like you to put them in order of importance. We can discuss your reasons for including each item and your reasons for putting the item in a particular order of importance.

BRINGING ORDER TO CHAOS

Children are far more receptive to learning a new skill when they see the value of the skill and are convinced that they can master the skill. The child who is chronically disorganized may need to be enticed into trying a new approach. Once convinced that the approach works, he can probably be won over. If the child is frontally assaulted, he most likely will be resistant and defensive.

If your child is highly disorganized, you might see yourself as a tennis coach who must transform a losing player into a winning player. As you model how things are done, you must provide guidance, feedback and repeated opportunity for practice. At the same time, you must provide support, encouragement and praise. Your goal is not only to improve your child's skills, but also to improve his self-image and self-confidence.

If you can help your child experience the benefits of effective time-management and organization, you can probably make him a convert. As he becomes increasingly time-efficient, he will begin to achieve at a level previously beyond his reach. With this new success, his self-esteem, self-confidence and Smartness Quotient will soar.

Chapter 6
Learning to Bounce Back

ANALYTICAL THINKING

David entered Kyle's room and pushed the door closed. It remained shut for an instant and then slowly swung open. Without thinking, the teenager pushed it closed again. And once again the door swung open. David shrugged, sat down on the bed next to Kyle, and began to discuss the party they were going to that evening. Other friends from school began to show up, and the same ritual occurred. They would push the door shut once or twice, and it would swing open. Like David, they would then quickly become preoccupied with the far more serious business of the party.

There were four teenagers in the room when Mark arrived. Like the others, he closed the door. As if on cue, it hit the jamb and slowly opened. Seeing this, Mark went to the door and began to examine the doorknob and the locking mechanism. He quickly discovered that the latch was stuck in such a way that the door could not possibly remain shut. After fiddling with the knob and exercising the spring mechanism several times, Mark closed the door again. This time it remained closed. He smiled and joined the others. The entire procedure had taken about 60 seconds.

LEARNING FROM MISTAKES

Put five teenagers together in a room, throw in the prospect of a party later that evening, and why in heaven's name would one kid be thinking about

156

the latch mechanism on an obstinate door? It was, as any teenager could clearly see, "no big deal."

Mark, however, saw it differently. When the door popped open, a buzzer went off in his mind. Something was wrong. Closed doors should remain closed. Mark's curiosity, analytical mind, sense of order and ingrained appreciation for the phenomenon of cause and effect compelled him to figure out why the door was defying logic. Once he investigated and assessed the source of the problem, he resolved it in less than a minute.

On the surface, Mark's response might not appear to be particularly significant. From his reaction, however, one might speculate how he might respond in other situations involving challenges, problems, mistakes or miscues. His response suggests that he probably possesses the following characteristics:

★ He is inquisitive.
★ He enjoys pitting his mind and skills against challenges.
★ He is deductive and logical.
★ He is thorough.
★ He is confident that he can remove obstacles that stand in his way.
★ He does not easily accept being thwarted.

From Mark's response, it would probably also be safe to infer that he is a good student and that he is conscientious and meticulous. These traits are the benchmarks of the smart thinker and the achiever.

Once convinced that a problem is solvable, children like Mark can become quite obsessed with overcoming the impediments standing in their way. A mistake or a setback is an invitation to a wrestling match. Feeling that they *deserve to prevail* and driven by egoism and a powerful achievement instinct, smart children typically persevere until they succeed or until they become convinced that there is no solution. These traits of curiosity, egoism, solution-oriented thinking, and stick-to-itiveness influence not only their reactions to major challenges but also their reactions to more mundane challenges. For example, one can imagine Mark at 9 years of age still working on a model airplane at 11 p.m. Fixated on finishing the job, he stops only when his parents insist that he go to bed.

The compelling need to understand, to make things work, and to pit one's abilities against obstacles distinguishes the achiever from the non-achiever or the underachiever. This need is a driving force shared by all who aspire to attain consummate proficiency in their chosen fields. One need only examine the *modus operandi* of the first-rate actor, writer, scientist, musician, dancer, film maker, scholar, or surgeon to appreciate that two common denominators—in addition to talent—set them apart: they learn from their mistakes and they avoid making the same mistakes repeatedly.

Mistakes are a fact of life—even smart children make them. The smart child, however, learns how to capitalize upon them. He doesn't persist in closing a door when reason dictates that something must be preventing the door from remaining shut.

Mark's confidence in his problem-solving skills was undoubtedly produced by positive problem-solving experiences. Because the not-so-smart child does not have the same experiences, he does not develop the same level of faith in himself. Less intellectually curious than the smart child, he does not learn as readily from his mistakes, and he tends to make the same mistakes over and over again.

Just as we could make some reasonable predictions about how Mark might react in other contexts, so can we make some predictions about how the other teenagers in Kyle's room might react. We might venture that:

★   They are not as inquisitive as Mark.
★   They do not derive the same level of enjoyment at the prospect of pitting their minds against challenges.
★   They are not as deductive and logical.
★   They are not as thorough.
★   They are not as confident that they can remove obstacles that stand in their way.
★   They are more willing to accept being thwarted.

These inferences are tentative, as it is possible that the teenagers in Kyle's room were simply so preoccupied with the party that they were uncharacteristically passive. However, if the inferences are accurate, the achievement level of the teenagers would most likely reflect their intellectual passivity.

Thinking smart is not an isolated event. Those who have developed the capacity to think actively and analytically use it continuously. It matters little whether they are studying, working or playing. Their minds are always operating on all eight cylinders.

RESISTING THE TEMPTATION TO GIVE UP

One of the results of a poor achievement track record is a tendency for a child to give up after making a mistake. Marginal success, low self-esteem, poor self-confidence, deficient intellectual curiosity and inadequate emotional resiliency produce profound feelings of incompetence.

Although a child's mistakes can be frustrating and demoralizing, they can provide an invaluable opportunity for the child to acquire insight about life and himself. For example, a child might run for class treasurer and lose the election. If she is smart and self-confident, she will probably rebound from her disappointment quickly. Sustained by her belief in herself, her abilities, and her "right" to attain her objective, she will begin a process of identifying the reasons for her defeat. She will seek feedback from her classmates, and she will go through a systematic process of self-assessment. Once she determines what went wrong, she will then make the necessary adjustments that will improve her chances of winning the next time, assuming she still wants the job. Through this process of trial, error and analysis, the smart child can "learn her lessons," capitalize on her reversal, and transform it into an opportunity for achieving success.

Contrast the behavior of the smart child who makes a mistake with that of the not-so-smart child. Lacking the capacity to think analytically, the not-so-smart child begins to spin his wheels. Because his self-confidence has already been undermined by imprinted negative associations with problem-solving, he interprets the new miscue as a further confirmation of his inadequacies. The net result is intensified stress, reinforced negative expectations and cerebral shutdown.

The child who lacks the capacity to capitalize on his mistakes must be helped to recognize that he has other options besides giving up. By training him to analyze problems and to link his errors in judgment with his performance (see "Cause and Effect" in Chapter 1), his parents can help him find the consistencies and inconsistencies in his behavior. By teaching him how to find the self-defeating common denominators that run through his thoughts, actions and responses to challenges, his parents can help him acquire greater insight into himself and his behavior. The child who persists in acting counterproductively, despite these efforts, will require professional counseling.

If a child is to avoid making the same mistakes repeatedly, he must become aware of his response patterns. The following checklist is designed to help you identify specific deficiencies in your child's reactions. A similar checklist for your child can be found later in the chapter.

Checklist for Parent
LEARNING FROM MISTAKES

Code: 0 = Never   1 = Rarely
      2 = Sometimes   3 = Often   5 = Always

My child becomes discouraged when he or she makes a mistake. _____

My child is afraid of making mistakes. _____

My child tends to give up if he or she makes a mistake. _____

My child makes the same mistake repeatedly. _____

My child fails to examine his or her mistakes. _____

My child does not perceive the common denominators that characterize his or her mistakes. _____

My child does not admit that he or she has made a mistake. _____

My child's judgment is deficient. _____

My child is defensive about mistakes. _____

My child is unwilling to discuss mistakes with me. _____

My child blames others for his mistakes. _____

TOTAL _____

Interpreting the Checklist

If your child's score is *above 20,* he is not responding constructively to mistakes. This tendency could create recurring problems. Specific activities designed to help your child respond more productively can be found later in this chapter.

HAVE I BEEN DOWN THIS ROAD BEFORE?

Even the non-analytical child *can* be taught to identify, classify and utilize

160

the data produced by life's inevitable miscues. This can be achieved by teaching the child a basic "learning from your mistakes formula." This formula, which children like Mark use reflexively, is central to analytical, solution-oriented thinking. The five steps include:

1. *Define the obvious.* (e.g., "A door should remain closed when shut.")
2. *Identify the mistake.* (e.g., "I have slammed this door closed twice, and it refuses to remain closed.")
3. *Investigate.* (e.g., "What could keep a door from remaining shut?")
4. *Explore corrective options.* (e.g., "I must somehow free up the latching mechanism.")
5. *Look for the common denominator.* (e.g., "When I encounter something that doesn't work, I usually get so frustrated that I either give up, break it because I'm angry, or make the same mistake over and over.")

You will note that these five steps parallel the DIBS System presented earlier. An additional step, however, has been added: *look for common denominator.* With sufficient practice, your child can begin to apply the five steps not only to solve such mundane problems as a troublesome door, but also to resolve major life crises.

Consider a child who has been caught in several lies that have caused him to lose credibility with his parents or his teacher. A far more effective alternative to lecturing him about lying would be for the child's parents to lead him through the formula. In so doing, they would be encouraging him to examine and consider the implications of lying. Achieving this insight into the implications of lying would have far more significant behavior-changing implications than simply impressing on the child that he will be punished if he is caught lying. Although punishment may be appropriate and necessary, it is not the primary objective. (Methods for guiding your child through the learning-from-your-mistakes formula are presented later in the chapter. One of the model dialogues specifically focuses on the issue of lying.)

Below you will find a checklist for your child to complete. This checklist should help your child identify his response patterns and can also serve as a catalyst for subsequent discussion.

LEARNING FROM MISTAKES CHECKLIST
For Child to Complete

Code: 0 = Never   1 = Rarely
       2 = Sometimes   3 = Often   4 = Always

I get discouraged when I make a mistake.   _____

I am afraid of making a mistake.   _____

I tend to give up when I make a mistake.   _____

I tend to make the same mistake over and over   _____
again.

I don't take the time to examine why I make   _____
mistakes.

I don't look for the common denominators that   _____
link my mistakes (Explain.)

I don't like to admit that I've made a mistake.   _____

I don't think carefully about what I am doing.   _____

I become defensive when I make a mistake.   _____
(Explain.)

I don't like to discuss my mistakes with my   _____
parents or teachers.

I tend to blame others for my mistakes.   _____

TOTAL   _____

Interpreting The Checklist with Your Child

You might explain the results of the checklist as follows: "A score *above 20* suggests that you would benefit from some of the activities in this chapter. Everybody make mistakes. I certainly do. The smart person, however, figures out how to learn from these mistakes and use them to advantage. Let's do some work together that can improve your skills in this area."

The following dialogue models how the five-step system for the learning-from-your-mistakes formula might be presented. An alternative, non-dialogue approach for presenting the formula is presented after the dialogue.

Model Dialogue #13
LEARNING FROM MISTAKES
Teenagers ages 13-17

Parent: I know that you're upset about our reaction to your having
              had a party while we were away for the weekend. We are

162

also upset, not only because you did something you were specifically forbidden to do, but also because you lied to us when we asked you if you had had a party. We decided to ground you and forbid you to use your car. It's time to discuss the situation calmly. Tell me your reaction to the punishment.

Teenager: It's unfair. Lots of kids have parties when their parents are away. The police didn't come. The neighbors didn't complain. Nothing is missing, nothing was broken, and nobody got drunk and rowdy. It was a quiet, private party. Only about 16 kids were here.

Parent: Let's not overlook the key issue: you did not have our permission to have a party when we were away. In fact, we specifically forbade you to have more than two visitors at any time during the weekend. You had permission to go out Saturday night with your friends, and you were supposed to be home by midnight. We felt that a 17-year-old was sufficiently responsible to be left alone for a weekend. Apparently we were wrong.

Teenager: I knew you'd be angry if I told you I had a party. It just sort of happened. I didn't plan it in advance.

Parent: But you allowed it to happen, despite our specifically forbidding it. This was unacceptable behavior, and you must deal with the consequences of your decision. We feel that our response is reasonable, and you will simply have to accept it. Do you think there are any lessons to be learned from this?

Teenager: What do you mean?

Parent: You made a decision which I think you agree was flawed. You got in trouble, and you have lost credibility with us. At the present time, it is difficult for us to have confidence in your judgment. What do you think you might do to regain our confidence?

Teenager: Not do anything like this again.

Parent: Do you say this simply because you would not like to get caught and be punished?

163

Teenager:	In part.
Parent:	Any other reasons?
Teenager:	I don't like the idea of your never trusting me again.
Parent:	Good point. There might be a time in your life when it will be very important for us to believe you, trust you and support you. Someone may accuse you of something you didn't do, and you may come to us for help. We want to be able to provide that help without reservation, but we must be able to trust you. What do you think you could do to regain our trust?
Teenager:	Prove to you that I can be trusted.
Parent:	I believe that you will re-establish trust. I think having the party was a great temptation, and you made an error in judgment. Have there been other times when you have been less than truthful with us?
Teenager:	Yes.
Parent:	I appreciate your forthrightness. In the past, we have pointed out several instances in which you have either bent the truth or withheld important information. At other times, we decided not to confront you. Perhaps that was a mistake on our part, and we will have to take a look at our reactions. I'm sure you see how dishonesty can seriously damage trust. You need to think about that the next time you might be tempted to mislead us. If dishonesty becomes a thread that runs through your relationship with us, everybody in the family is going to suffer. Do you agree?
Teenager:	Yes.
Parent:	I feel confident you'll handle similar situations better in the future. I also think that you will be straight with us, even if you have done something wrong and might have to experience the consequences. You can regain our trust by being responsible during the next few months. Everyone makes mistakes and errors in judgment. The smart person learns from them and doesn't make them again.

164

The parent in the preceding dialogue clearly expresses his disappointment and upset about his son's behavior. Although he is distressed, he
recognizes that his primary objective is to change his son's behavior and
not to punish or lecture him. With this goal in mind, he leads the teenager
through the five steps of the previously described "learning-from-your-
mistakes" formula *(identify the mistake, define the obvious, examine the
situation, explore corrective options* and *find a common denominator).*

Although the father is direct, he does not preach. He does, however,
unequivocally communicate his position on the key issues to his son. He
intentionally ends the discussion on a positive note and assures the teenager that he can re-establish trust by acting responsibly and forthrightly in
the future. By expressing confidence in his son's ability to learn from his
errors in judgment, he provides him with an important affirmation at a
time when he is undoubtedly feeling unhappy and upset.

As you read the dialogue, you might be thinking that it is not easy to
remain calm and rational when your child has broken an important rule.
This is precisely why the assessment process should take place after the
"smoke has cleared." In the dialogue, the parents have already decided on
the punishment, and the discussion occurs after this decision has been
made. An alternative approach that deals with the same issue and applies
the five steps of the learning-from-your-mistakes formula is presented
below.

Supplemental Activity
LEARNING FROM MISTAKES
Teenagers ages 13-17

Situation:	You're upset about being punished for having a party while we were away. We're also upset. I'd like to deal with the issues in a way that will not lead to an argument. Are you willing to work on it with me? Let's do it step by step.
Identifying the Mistake:	Now that you've had some time to think about what happened, I think we can look at the events calmly. What do you think caused this upset? OK. Now let me tell you my assessment of the situation. Would you agree that you did something that violated the rules and that undermined our trust in you?

Define the Obvious:

Tell me in your own words what you can conclude and what you have learned from this event. OK. Now let me put it in my words: you cannot break the rules of this family without getting into trouble and facing the consequences. To allow you to break the rules would be a failure on our part as responsible parents. Do you understand the reasoning behind this?

Explore Corrective Action:

How can you re-establish our trust? How do you think you might respond to similar situations in the future?

Identify Common Denominators:

Have there been other cases in which you have bent the truth? You don't need to list them, but I am curious if you can identify a common denominator in your responses to certain situations? You know what it means to find a common denominator in math. You look for a number that is shared in common by all of the fractions. The same concept applies to life. For instance, when you feel that we are unfair or unreasonable in our demands, do you think that this conclusion would justify your misleading us? Could this be a common denominator? Aren't you on safer ground when you tell us about your concerns?.

Think about how you might deal with a similar situation if it should arise again. Think specifically about how you could handle it without having to bend the truth or withhold information that we should know. Also, think about what you might do if you are upset with a family rule or a decision we make. Would you be willing to share your feelings openly and would you be willing to examine with us our reasons for the rule or the decision? I'd like you to consider these issues the next time you are faced with a major decision that could involve

breaking a family rule. I think you realize that some
day it may be very important that we believe and
trust you. If you do not have our trust, we may not
be willing to go out on a limb and provide the
support you might desperately need.

HELPING YOUR CHILD
BOUNCE BACK FROM SETBACKS

A child must not only be able to learn from his mistakes, he must also be
able to rebound from setbacks. Possessing this resiliency is a requisite to
achievement and a vital survival mechanism.

Smart children prefer to avoid setbacks whenever possible. When they
do experience a reversal, they realize that they must pick up the pieces,
rearrange them so they fit, and get on with the task at hand. Whereas the
not-so-smart, insecure child generally perceives setbacks as a confirmation
of his inadequacies, the smart, self-confident child recognizes that setbacks
can be a springboard for ultimate success.

The not-so-smart child, and especially the emotionally fragile child, can
be devastated by a series of reversals. Even an isolated setback can cause
him to become emotionally paralyzed. Resigned to failure and lacking
emotional resiliency, he would instinctively try to avoid any situation that
could expose him to another defeat.

The following checklist will help you determine whether or not your
child is rebounding effectively from reversals. It will also help you identify
specific counterproductive behavior patterns that could undermine your
child's capacity to achieve.

Checklist for Parent
BOUNCING BACK FROM SETBACKS

Code: 0 = Never 1 = Rarely
      2 = Sometimes 3 = Often 4 = Always

My child gets very discouraged when he suffers   _____
a setback.

My child is tempted to give up when he fails at   _____
something.

My child tries to avoid things that are difficult.   _____

167

My child is convinced he is dumb when he has a _____
setback.

My child regrets having tried something when _____
he doesn't do well.

My child believes people think less of him if _____
they know he has failed at something.

My child doesn't like to admit that he has had a _____
setback.

My child wants to run away and hide after a _____
failure.

When my child is doing something that becomes _____
too difficult, he quits.

My child is unwilling to ask for help. _____

When my child encounters difficulty, he gets so _____
frustrated that he can no longer work efficiently.

If my child is forced to ask for help, he becomes _____
defensive.

TOTAL _____

Interpreting the Checklist

A score *above 22* suggests that your child is not responding effectively to
setbacks. This response pattern could create major barriers to achievement.

Obviously, setbacks are not pleasant experiences for anyone. Parents
who perceive that these setbacks are producing excessive sensitivity,
frustration, anxiety and stress have justifiable cause for concern and must
intervene. A system for improving your child's "Bounce-back Quotient"
and for developing a more productive pattern of responses to setbacks is
explored below.

Before you examine the issue of rebounding from setbacks and begin
the activities, ask your child to complete the checklist for children. This
checklist is designed to help your child gain insight into how he or she is
handling reversals.

Checklist for Child
SETBACKS

Code: 0 = Never   1 = Rarely
       2 = Sometimes   3 = Often   4 = Always

I get very discouraged when I have a setback.   _____

I feel like giving up when I fail at something.   _____

I try to avoid doing something that is difficult   _____
for me.

I feel dumb when I have a setback.   _____

I regret having tried something when I did not   _____
do well.

I think people think less of me if they know I   _____
have failed at something.

I don't like to admit that I have had a setback.   _____

I want to run away and hide after a failure.   _____

If I am doing something and it gets too difficult,   _____
I quit.

I don't like to ask for help.   _____

When I run into difficulty, I get so frustrated   _____
that I can no longer work efficiently.

If I have to ask for help, I feel stupid.   _____

TOTAL   _____

Interpreting the Checklist

Explain to your child that a score *above 22* suggests that some work needs to be done in the area of developing more effective responses to setbacks. The checklist can also be used as a catalyst for discussion of the issues raised.

SHARING YOUR OWN PAINFUL EXPERIENCES
If your child is to develop emotional resiliency in the face of a setback, he

169

must ultimately accept that setbacks are an inescapable part of the human condition. Although he may feel discouraged, the child must be helped to realize that he has two key choices: he can allow himself to be crushed, or he can use the reversal as a catapult. Specific dialogues that model how to guide your child toward this realization and how to help your child develop more positive responses to setbacks can be found later in the chapter.

A particularly effective method for reducing the fears, inhibitions, phobias, defensiveness and demoralization that can result when a child experiences a setback is for you to share personal experiences in your own life. By sharing these painful moments and by describing how your own emotional resources were tested, you are helping your child appreciate that sadness and disappointment in the face of a setback are common. At the same time, you are demonstrating that a positive, solution-oriented response to a reversal is possible. Your ultimate goal is to help your child develop a different perspective. Once he understands that everyone is occasionally sidetracked, he can begin to appreciate how important it is that he learn to handle these roadblocks successfully.

In the following dialogue, a parent examines a personal setback with a younger child. He helps his son put his own setback in a more positive perspective, and he shows him how he can learn from it and how he can use his newfound wisdom constructively.

Model Dialogue #14
BOUNCING BACK FROM SETBACKS
Children ages 7-12

Parent: I received a note from your teacher. She thinks that you would make more progress if she moved you into a lower reading group. How do you feel about this?

Child: I don't care.

Parent: Really?

Child: I don't care!

Parent: I know that you've been struggling to keep up with your reading group. Do you think this will make it easier for you?

Child: I know I can't read good.

Parent: How does that make you feel?

Child:	Dumb.
Parent:	Dumb?
Child:	If I were smart, I could read good.
Parent:	I'd like to change the subject for a few minutes and talk to you about baseball.
Child:	What does baseball have to do with it?
Parent:	We'll see. When I was in high school, I wanted to be on the baseball team more than anything in the world. Unfortunately, I wasn't a very good athlete. Nevertheless, I was determined to make the team. When I tried out in my freshman year, I was rejected. The coach didn't even offer to put me on the junior varsity. I was crushed. I went home, went to my room, closed the door, and spent the whole afternoon feeling miserable. At dinner, my dad asked me what was wrong. I told him, and I expected him to give me a lot of sympathy. He simply said, "I'm sorry you didn't make the team. I guess you've got your work cut out for you." I told him I never wanted to play baseball again, and he said that that was my choice. He also told me that I could choose to learn how to play better. He said he felt confident that I would make the second choice because he knew I wasn't a quitter.
Child:	What did you do?
Parent:	I thought about what my dad had said, and I realized he was right. After I got over my disappointment, I spent every free minute practicing.
Child:	What happened?
Parent:	The next season I tried out again. And again, I didn't make the varsity, but the coach agreed to put me on the junior varsity. I was the only tenth-grader on junior varsity, and it was a little embarrassing to be with all those ninth-graders. But I didn't care. I had my uniform, and despite the fact that I was still not a very good player, I did get to play in most of the games.
Child:	How did you feel knowing you weren't a very good player?
Parent:	Well, I wanted to be better, but I was still happy simply to be playing. About 2 months later, one of the kids on the varsity

broke his ankle, and the coach moved me up. I guess he selected me because I was the oldest and because he liked my attitude. I really worked hard in practice. I was always the first one on the field and the last one in the locker room. Although I had played second base on the junior varsity, the coach made me a reserve outfielder on the varsity. That first year on the varsity, I sat on the bench, but I tried to hustle more than anyone on the team during practice and during the pregame warm-ups. In eleventh grade, I played in only two games. In my senior year, I played about half the time. During the last game of the year, the coach sent me in as a pinch-hitter in the bottom of the ninth inning. It was a tie game, and if we won the game we would finish with a winning record for the year. Our team hadn't had a winning season for 5 years. I don't know why the coach chose me to pinch hit. I certainly wasn't a power hitter. I suppose he felt that I was so eager that he owed it to me. I got a single and drove in the winning run. It was one of the biggest thrills of my life.

Child: Did the guys on the team go crazy?

Parent: You bet they did! I was the big hero at the victory dance. You know, what happened to me also happens all the time in the majors. A professional baseball player can go through a stretch in which he is not playing very well. His manager may decide to send him down to the minors for a while until he can improve his skills. If you were a pro player and were sent down, what would you do?

Child: What do you mean?

Parent: Would you quit?

Child: No.

Parent: But you've been sent down to the minors.

Child: So? Players get sent down all the time. If they work hard, they can come back.

Parent: You're right. But do you think the player would be upset and discouraged by being sent down?

Child: Yes.

Parent: But he wouldn't give up, would he?

172

Child:	No.
Parent:	Do you see any similarities between the baseball player and your situation in school?
Child:	You mean that I could work hard and maybe get back into a higher reading group.
Parent:	Exactly. You can choose not to let being "sent down to the minors" destroy your confidence, or you could do what you need to do to work your way back. Perhaps you could get some good coaching from a tutor. What do you think?
Child:	OK.
Parent:	Should we try to get you a good reading coach?
Child:	Yeah.

It is quite understandable that the child in the preceding dialogue would feel discouraged about being moved to a lower reading group. Recognizing this, his father strategically guides his son toward a realization that setbacks are a fact of life and helps him appreciate that he is not alone in experiencing defeat. By linking the child's setback to a reversal he himself experienced in school, the father demonstrates that there are productive ways to assess and respond to negative events in life. Appreciating the value of actively involving his son in the discussion/examination process, he then selects a sports analogy to which his son can easily relate. The metaphor of the professional baseball player being sent down to the minors helps the child appreciate that the athlete, although obviously disappointed, can choose to perfect his skills and work his way back up. The parallel is obvious: if the child wants to work his way into a higher reading group, he can. But first he must learn how to use the temporary setback as an opportunity for growth.

In the dialogue below, a mother examines a similar issue with her teenage daughter. She, too, shares a setback that she has personally experienced. She explores her feelings and her disappointment and describes how she handled the situation. You will note that the mother carefully avoids any temptation to play an "ain't I wonderful" role.

Model Dialogue #15
BOUNCING BACK FROM SETBACKS
Teenagers ages 13-17

Parent: I imagine you're real disappointed that you didn't get the part you wanted in the play.

Teenager: I tried so hard. I don't know why I wasn't chosen.

Parent: It's upsetting to take a risk and then to experience a setback.

Teenager: I'm never going to try out again. I don't want to act anymore.

Parent: I know the temptation to give up is really strong when you are feeling rejected. I've felt the same way several times in my own life.

Teenager: You did?

Parent: Yes. When I graduated from college, I decided that I wanted to live in San Francisco. I came out to the West Coast looking for a job. I saw an ad in the paper for a position as a trainee in advertising with a well-known corporation. After the initial interview, I knew that I wanted the job really badly. I was then asked to take a battery of tests. One test was a psychological test. I had studied psychology in college, and I felt that I could "see through" many of the questions. I decided to try to impress them with how cute and clever I was. One particular question asked me what I dreamed or fantasized about. I wrote that I fantasized about being a queen and that everybody had to take orders from me. Perhaps I was rejected for the job because I was too clever or perhaps there were other reasons. Nevertheless, I didn't get the job, and I was terribly disappointed. For a while I was in shock. Then I got mad at myself for being so crushed by the rejection and at them for being so stupid. I decided that I would get an even better job.

Teenager: How long were you sad?

Parent: A couple of days.

Teenager: What did you do then?

Parent: I decided to go to graduate school. Once I got an advanced degree, getting a good job was a cinch.

Teenager: Do you think if I tried out again, I might get a part?

Parent: I think so. But I think you need to talk to the director and find out why you weren't selected and what you could do to improve your skills. If I'm not mistaken, the next school play is in the spring. Perhaps if you could find out what they are going to put on, you could begin preparing now. If you're real serious, perhaps we could even enroll you in a drama class at the local children's theater. Would you like that?

Teenager: Yes!

Although the mother in the preceding dialogue acknowledges that setbacks cause pain and disappointment, she does not lose sight of her primary objective and carefully guides her daughter to a realization that she has choices in responding to setbacks:

★   She can give up.
★   She can continue to struggle.
★   She can figure out a clever plan to neutralize the setback and reduce the chances of it occurring again.

By describing her response, the mother helps her child appreciate that the last two options are the most strategic. Rather than simply commiserate with her daughter, she suggests a practical strategy that could improve her daughter's chances of getting a part in the school play the next time she tries out. In this way, she actively involves the teenager in the process of developing a solution-oriented game plan. The mother realizes that her role is to guide her child to a key insight: smart thinking and resiliency can transform a setback and a disappointment into an opportunity for growth.

DEVELOPING YOUR CHILD'S BOUNCE-BACK QUOTIENT

When you encourage your child to examine his responses systematically and when you show him how to develop alternative and more productive responses, you are helping him improve his "BBQ" (Bounce-back Quotient). This examination/alternative strategy approach can significantly reduce the anticipatory and often paralyzing anxiety that your child might experience when he contemplates having to deal with situations that have previously caused him frustration and pain.

175

Encouraging your child to analyze problems does not imply that the examination process is exclusively intellectual. Your child must also be encouraged to look at his feelings. If he is frightened, he must be helped to express and examine his fear. Leading your child through this process requires an extra measure of gentleness, sensitivity and patience. You must recognize that it is often very difficult and embarrassing for a child (or an adult) to acknowledge his innermost feelings. The temptation to "circle the wagons" and protect oneself from one's vulnerabilities and inadequacies is especially compelling when a child is feeling frightened and insecure. If the examination/alternative strategy method is to be successful, it must deal with the emotional issues. It's one thing for a child to explore issues on an cerebral level. It's quite another for him to explore feelings on a visceral level, confront the emotional barriers, and then get on with the job of resolving the problem.

Before your child would be willing to share his deeper feelings with you, he must trust you. He must be convinced that you will respond non-judgmentally and with sensitivity. For example, he might say: "The other kids don't like me because I am terrible in sports. No one wants me on their team, and I always get picked last." If you were to say, "That's silly," you would be trivializing his perceptions and feelings. Were you to respond, "Don't let it bother you if they laugh," you would also be failing to provide your child with substantive support as he struggles to handle a very real crisis in his life. Despite good intentions, your reaction would not help your child feel more competent and secure. A far more effective response would be to help your child analyze the issues, sort out his feelings about the rejection and brainstorm some workable solutions to the problem.

If your child is to survive and prevail in a competitive world he must develop his Bounce-Back Quotient. He must realize that there are effective alternatives to shutting down, developing phobias and spinning wheels. With sufficient practice, your child can begin to internalize solution-oriented thinking skills. As he becomes increasingly adept at solving problems and as his self-esteem and self-confidence grow, he will be far less vulnerable to life's setbacks.

THE EFFECTS OF FEAR

Fear is an important survival mechanism. In life-threatening situations, it can produce a surge of adrenalin that can make the difference between life and death.

Fear also serves children in other, seemingly less extreme situations. It can dissuade a child from walking down a dark alley in an unsafe area, from

176

talking to a stranger oɩ the street or from climbing on an unsafe rock pile.

Fear also has a negative side. When it is irrational, based upon distortions in perception, or thɛ result of negative associations that have been psychologically imprinted on the child's psyche, it can paralyze a child physically and emotionally. A second-grader, for example, may feel embarrassed by her poor oral reading skills and may try to avoid reading aloud whenever possible. Each time she is asked to read in front of the class by her teacher, she becomes frightened and self-conscious and this anxiety magnifies her reading problems. Convinced that she is hopelessly inadequate in reading, she will read only when forced by circumstances to do so. If the underlying problem is not resolved, the child's lack of confidence, her negative mind-set about her ability, her low level of emotional resiliency and her fear cannot help but affect her subsequent career choices and produce monumental psychological barriers to achievement.

The child with specific, identifiable deficits must obviously be given appropriate assistance. But this assistance may not be sufficient. She must also be helped to discover that there are strategies that can reduce her vulnerability and her fears about exposing herself to real or imagined failure and ridicule. Once she learns how to think smart, she will realize that there are viable alternatives to allowing herself to become emotionally crippled by temporary setbacks.

STICK-TO-ITIVENESS

It is always satisfying and gratifying when one's endeavors go according to plan, when all of the pieces fit together neatly, and when there is a smooth progression and a predictable and positive outcome. Smart children experience this satisfaction far more frequently than not-so-smart children. Their ability to make their endeavors go according to plan is primarily attributable to the fact that smart children *have a plan* and are willing to stick to it until they become convinced that it either cannot work or that a better plan is available.

Even the best plans, however, occasionally lead to detours or obstacles. All children—the smart ones and the not-so-smart ones—inevitably encounter "glitches." Sometimes the impediments are minor and are quickly overcome. In other instances, the barriers may appear insurmountable. Under such circumstances, the ultimate outcome often hinges on the child's stick-to-itiveness.

The capacity to persevere in the face of an obstacle or a reversal is another of the distinguishing characteristics of the smart child. For example, a child might begin a project in the shop. He decides what he wants to build and cuts out the pieces, but when it comes time to glue the pieces together, he discovers to his dismay that they don't fit. As he struggles, he becomes increasingly frustrated. He begins to force the joints together, and they break. Finally, he throws the pieces into the garbage pail. At the critical juncture in the process, the child reached a crisis point: the pieces wouldn't fit. He was then faced with some key decisions:

1. He could give up.
2. He could become angry, upset and incapacitated.
3. He could put the project aside temporarily in order to see things more clearly.
4. He could re-examine his original plan for the project to determine where the miscalculation occurred.
5. He could assess the problem analytically and make the necessary adjustments in his planning and execution.
6. He could ask for assistance.

The child who selects any of the last four choices is obviously thinking smart. Unfortunately, many children select choice one or two.

The parents of the not-so-smart child often find themselves enmeshed in a predictable script. They repeatedly admonish their child to develop stick-to-itiveness, but despite their efforts, they discover to their dismay that their child refuses to change his behavior. The typical outcome of these encounters is an argument, hurt feelings and resentment.

Stick-to-itiveness does not materialize on demand. For a child to persevere in the face of a challenge, a setback, or a mistake, he must be convinced that he possesses the resources to find solutions to his problems. The child who forces the pieces together, breaks them, and then throws them in the garbage pail is clearly not convinced of his ability to overcome obstacles by means of smart thinking and perseverance.

Confidence in one's ability to prevail in the face of a major obstacle is a result of having experienced success handling similar challenging situations. The child who is willing to persevere has already proven to himself his own efficacy and potency. He has built things and has made them fit together. This creates a paradox. To persevere in the face of an obstacle, a child needs to have experienced success. But to experience success, a child must be able to persevere.

The solution to the paradox is obvious. The parents of a child with a low perseverance threshold must carefully groom their child so that he can begin to experience success. They must purposefully set time aside when they can build things with their child, and they must carefully model how to plan projects so that the pieces will fit together. Should the child encounter an impediment, experience a setback or make a mistake, he must be trained to examine these events calmly and systematically. If the problem doesn't yield to his efforts, he must be encouraged to put the work aside until he can approach the challenge with a clearer mind. The child must also be trained to develop solution-oriented strategies that capitalize on the wisdom he has gained from past experiences. This process must be repeated and repeated (at intervals and with time out!) until it becomes standard operating procedure.

Your child cannot be lectured into developing stick-to-itiveness. He has to see its value in helping him achieve his objectives. He must become convinced that perseverance is more than self-discipline for self-discipline's sake. With skill and patience, his parents must guide him to the realization that perseverance, when coupled with smart thinking, can produce results that are enjoyable and satisfying. Once your child discovers that productive behavior can significantly increase the amount of pleasure he experiences, he will have acquired a powerful incentive for thinking analytically, for learning from his mistakes and for persevering in the face of a setback.

Chapter 7
Putting It All Together

HE NEEDED DATA

Jason's voice radiated confidence and maturity. Although I was delighted to hear from him, I was surprised by the telephone call, as I hadn't spoken with the teenager in almost 5 years.

Jason informed me that he was in the process of applying to colleges and wanted some advice. Despite having received mostly B's in honors courses and a grade point average of 3.1, he was apprehensive about selecting appropriate colleges.

I was very familiar with Jason's high school. It offered an excellent honors program, and Jason had taken some of the school's most challenging courses. His grade point average was all the more remarkable when one considered that he had struggled throughout elementary school and junior high school with a relatively severe learning disability.

As a seventh-grader, Jason had received approximately 2 hours per week of intensive, specialized remedial help at our learning center. The program lasted approximately 12 months, and after making remarkable progress, he discontinued with our blessing at the beginning of eighth grade. Initial reports from his junior high school indicated that the 13-year-old was doing fine and contact with the family ended.

When Jason entered high school, he realized that he still had some residual learning deficits. Because he read slowly and had difficulty memorizing information, he found studying very challenging. To compensate, he had studied a minimum of 3-1/2 hours each school night

180

throughout 4 years of high school. Finding this much time in his schedule had been a major accomplishment, for the teenager also played three varsity sports.

As one of the top gymnasts in California, Jason was all but assured of an athletic scholarship to many of the top schools in the country. In fact, several university coaches had already contacted him and had informed him that a scholarship was guaranteed. Nevertheless, Jason was very concerned about choosing a school that might prove too academically demanding. He knew himself well enough to realize that if he did not do well academically, he would become discouraged and demoralized.

The lingering effects of Jason's learning problems were underscored by his relatively low scores on the SAT (Scholastic Achievement Test). In his junior year, his combined total for the two sections of the test was 910 out of a possible score of 1600. Despite these scores, there was no doubt in my mind that Jason was highly intelligent. There was also no doubt in my mind about his willingness to work. His grade point average clearly reflected his conscientiousness.

Jason's SAT scores, however, caused me to share his concerns about selecting the appropriate university. Although a firm believer in the value of struggling to prevail over obstacles, I could see no benefit in the teenager beating his head against the wall. It was clear that if he was to do well academically, he would have to select a college that provided tutorial assistance. He would also have to select a school whose curriculum was reasonable for a student with his level of academic skills and his history of learning problems.

As we talked, Jason's analytical thinking skills became very apparent. He had defined his goals and had carefully considered the issues. Realizing that he needed professional advice, he had called me without any prompting from his parents. He was very aware of his strengths and weaknesses, and although he wanted to attend the best school possible, he also wanted to make sure that his choice was realistic.

At the end of our telephone conversation, I made three specific recommendations:

1. That I administer a battery of tests to determine his current skill level in specific areas.
2. That Jason apply for authorization to take the SAT again untimed. (This option is reserved for students with documented learning disabilities. To qualify, Jason would need substantiation from me and his high school).
3. That he set up an appointment with a private college admissions

advisor who could help him examine the entrance requirements at each school he was considering.

The admissions advisor was knowledgable about the entrance and curriculum requirements at the schools he was considering, and she would be able to advise him whether or not learning support and tutoring programs were available. (Because of severe budget cuts, Jason's high school had eliminated its college counseling program.)

Jason and his parents concurred with my recommendations, and we made an appointment for the testing battery. As I suspected, the tests revealed that Jason's skills were slightly to moderately below grade level in several key areas. The deficiencies that concerned me most involved reading comprehension and written language expression. I knew that deficits in these areas could create major obstacles for Jason in college.

When we met to discuss the results of the tests, Jason's questions were focused and penetrating. As we explored the pros and cons of choosing a school with a rigorous academic curriculum versus one with less-demanding standards, he expressed his concerns and shared his thoughts and feelings without hesitation. I provided as much information as I could, and I knew that Jason would carefully consider this information and factor it into his final decision. The next step in the decision-making process would be a conference with the college admissions counselor.

Jason's score on the untimed SAT improved by over 120 points. After much soul-searching, he ultimately selected an excellent university that offered a comprehensive learning-assistance program. Jason is optimistic that he can maintain a B average, and he is equally optimistic that he will someday represent the United States in the Olympics.

PUSHING THE SMART-THINKING BUTTON

The youngster who wants to succeed in a highly competitive world must not only acquire a wide spectrum of academic, vocational and thinking skills, he must also learn how, when and where to apply these skills. Specific behaviors signal that a child has acquired the resources requisite to achievement. These include the ability to:

* evaluate the available information
* assess options
* establish goals and priorities
* organize time and resources
* develop a strategy for achieving objectives
* persevere in the face of obstacles

182

* learn from mistakes
* bounce back from setbacks
* assess oneself objectively.

The smart child learns to use his analytical-thinking skills like a scalpel. With deftness, he cuts through the surrounding tissue, exposes the underlying problem or challenge and does what is necessary to fix it.

In responding to his dilemma, Jason capitalized on all of his analytical-thinking skills. He realized that he needed information to make intelligent decisions, and he called me because I had originally diagnosed his learning problem and had supervised his remedial program. Realizing that he was faced with decisions that could profoundly affect his future, Jason understood that he would have to assess himself and his situation carefully and objectively.

Smart children are practical. They know they possess a cerebral "turbocharger." They also know that if they are to shift into overdrive and make it up the hill, they must activate the turbocharger by pushing their "smart-thinking" button.

Not-so-smart children do not know where their smart-thinking button is located. Even if they could find it, they would probably discover that it is not connected. Because they have not developed their analytical-thinking skills, they do not perceive the cause-and-effect relationship that links the quality of their thinking processes with the quality of the results they attain. If they are to function more effectively, these children must be taught how to string and attach the wire that links the smart-thinking button to their brain. Those who do not are destined to continue performing marginally.

Pushing the smart-thinking button sometimes demands a conscious, measured decision by a child to draw upon his problem-solving skills. In other situations, the child may push the button reflexively. A stimulus—such as a door that doesn't close properly—can trigger an immediate smart-thinking response. Reacting instinctively, the child immediately begins to search for the source of the problem.

Jason's response to his dilemma about college was deliberate, and his decision to think strategically was conscious and intentional. He used every smart-thinking technique in his arsenal. His strategy followed a classic problem-solving progression:

1. What is my objective?
2. What data do I need to achieve my objective?
3. How do I get the data?

4. How can I best use this data?
5. What have I learned from similar situations and what do I already know about myself?
6. Who or what can assist me to reach my objective?
7. What should my strategy be?
8. How can I best implement this strategy?

You will note that this progression is quite similar to the one used by Jeremy, the 10-year-old described in Chapter 1 who wanted to carry the camping gear to the campsite in one trip. The parallels should come as no surprise. With minor deviations, human beings have been using this same analytical problem-solving progression since they first became capable of conscious thought.

The child who has acquired an effective problem-solving system has a powerful competitive edge over the child who does not have access to such a system. Because he knows how to use his smart-thinking button, he can begin to take charge of his own destiny.

RELEVANCY HOOKS

When a child is doing something that is important to him, he has a natural incentive for extra effort, perseverance, planning and smart thinking. The power of relevancy can be seen in the behavior of the child who identifies something that he wants very badly and then proceeds with single-minded purpose to attain his objective.

Imagine a teenager who wants to go skiing with her friends over the weekend. If she is astute, she knows in advance what objections her parents might raise. They will ask her if she will have her homework assignments completed for Monday. They will want to know where she will be staying and if she has enough money to pay for lift tickets, food and lodging. And of course, they will want to be certain that there will be a parent along to chaperone.

If the teenager has not considered these issues before talking to her parents and if she is not able to respond appropriately to their concerns, it is unlikely that they will permit her to go on the trip. If she anticipates their concerns and plans her responses in advance, she significantly improves her chances of attaining her objective. Her strategic planning not only allows her to get what she wants in this particular situation, it also "scores points" that can be used when she seeks her parents' approval for other projects and ideas. Because she thinks smart, she recognizes that once she convinces her parents that she is responsible and level-headed, they will

184

trust her and probably give her the benefit of the doubt the next time she wants something.

The intuitively smart child realizes the benefits of planning, responsible behavior and analytical thinking. In contrast, the non-intuitively smart child must be taught to appreciate these benefits.

Personal gain is a powerful motivation for smart thinking. The child who is working for a payoff generates natural self-discipline, diligence, motivation, responsibility and stick-to-itiveness, and he does so without needing to be lectured, coerced or threatened with punishment. It matters little whether the payoff is a skiing trip, a varsity football letter, a new bicycle or a good grade. What matters is that the child truly desires the payoff.

The child who realizes that he can improve the quality of his life and get what he wants by thinking smart has achieved insight that can profoundly affect his life. Once he identifies what he wants and commits himself to achieving it, he has a compelling, self-serving reason for developing and utilizing his physical and intellectual resources.

Wise parents (and teachers) who want to improve a child's performance recognize that active, voluntary involvement invariably changes human performance. By intentionally creating relevancy "hooks," by making projects and undertakings as meaningful and engaging as possible, and by helping the child perceive the value of what he is doing or being asked to do, they can transform resistance, procrastination and passivity into quality participation. These parents and teachers have realized a basic truth about human behavior: a child who is helped to recognize the potential benefit from his endeavors has a powerful incentive to improve the quality of his work.

To appreciate this phenomenon, imagine a typical teenager's resistance and procrastination when asked by his parents to wash the family car. Compare this reaction with his behavior when he himself decides to wash the car because he has a date with a special girl.

The ultimate goal is for a child to begin creating (and even contriving) his own relevancy hooks without his parents or teachers having to guide him. Of course, not every undertaking is intrinsically meaningful and engaging. Emptying the trash or mowing the lawn may never become more than a chore. Nevertheless, the smart child recognizes that there are benefits in doing the chore responsibly. By doing the work without fussing, the child realizes he can avoid unpleasant repercussions and can earn his parents' appreciation.

Sometimes the value of a particular undertaking is very obvious to a child. For example, a teenager who doesn't have the money to have his transmission overhauled at a garage has a compelling reason to learn how to do the job himself. If he is sufficiently desperate to get his car in working order, he will recognize that he must study the repair manual before he begins. As he dismantles the transmission, he quickly realizes he will not be able to put the transmission back together unless he organizes his materials and tools and carefully plans his steps. Although he may make mistakes, he will learn from them, and if he runs into a problem he cannot handle, he will ask for help from someone more knowledgeable. Because he has a vested interest in thinking and acting smart, the teenager will take these steps on his own without having to be admonished or reminded.

Sometimes the relevancy of an undertaking is not obvious to a child. In such instances, parents and teachers may need to brainstorm with the child ways to make the project or assignment more meaningful. For example, students in a tenth-grade history class might be assigned to write a report about the Founding Fathers and the significance of the Federalist Papers. At first glance, the social and economic conditions that led to the War of Independence might not appear especially relevant, and many students might perceive the assignment as simply another boring academic exercise. Recognizing this, the talented teacher would engage her students' interest by relating the issues that concerned the Founding Fathers to issues that directly affect her students. She might ask the class to consider how they would respond if our government had laws that permitted citizens to be thrown into prison without charges being brought or without a trial being held. By making the principles relevant and by encouraging her students to think actively about the issues, she improves both the quality of their participation and the quality of their understanding.

Students who discover on their own how to make their studies more meaningful have an obvious advantage over those who do not. This is especially true when they find themselves in classes taught by boring, non-creative teachers.

The difference in the performance of a child who is actively involved and that of a child who is passively involved can be startling. Contrast the work of an 11-year-old who is asked by his mother to strip the wax off the kitchen floor with that of the same child who is engrossed in assembling a new radio-controlled toy car that he just bought with his own money. Or compare an imaginative 11-year-old's essay about life on a space station in the 21st century with the same child's essay about colonial farming methods. Although a talented teacher might make the subject of farming methods interesting and engaging, she would probably be the first to acknowledge that a space station is intrinsically more interesting to children in our society than colonial farming methods.

186

Like their adult counterparts, kids do their best work and their best thinking when they find value and pleasure in what they are doing. It should be noted, however, that the smart child recognizes the value of getting a good grade on an essay irrespective of how uninteresting the subject might be and would probably do a good job despite not being particularly enthused about the subject.

The not-so-smart child usually considers any undertaking that does not produce immediate pleasure or an immediate payoff to be a chore. At best, he participates reluctantly and passively. At worst, he is resistant. The net result of the child's marginal involvement is marginal performance.

The acid test for determining if a child has learned to engage himself in what he is doing occurs when he is faced with the prospect of doing something uninteresting. If the child recognizes that it is to his advantage to do well and can figure out on his own how to make the undertaking relevant and engaging, he has passed the test. His ability to create or contrive a relevancy hook testifies that he has learned how to push his smart-thinking button.

Once a child discovers that relevancy and active involvement are his allies and can help him achieve his objective, he will begin to seek and create relevancy without having to be prodded or coerced. If the previously described teenager with the faulty transmission were to apply the same analytical thinking and planning skills he uses to repair his car to improving his grades, he might conceivably become a straight A student.

Quality performance in any endeavor is a function of four characteristics: innate ability, effort, skill and desire. Fortunately, the last three characteristics can be developed, and in many situations, they can more than compensate for the lack of innate ability.

CLASSIFYING INFORMATION AND EXPERIENCES

On both a conscious and unconscious level, children are continually filtering and distilling their life experiences. The process produces wisdom, insight and good judgment. Like cognac distilled from champagne, this knowledge must be carefully stored for future use.

The previous metaphor unfortunately breaks down at this point, for unlike cognac, wisdom, insight, and judgment cannot be stored in a cool cellar. Rather, they must be stored in the attic where the child's "cerebral computer" is located. Here acquired knowledge, information and understanding are classified and filed for future reference.

As a child learns more about life and about himself through experience and formal education, he adds to his data base. He develops the capacity to

187

identify the relationships that exist between what he is currently learning and what he has already learned. The wisdom on file allows him to make associations, find common threads and predict outcomes.

For example, the child may have ordered several products through the mail and may have been disappointed by what she has received. If she is thinking smart, she will draw conclusions from these experiences and will consider them before ordering something new from a catalogue. This procedure of carefully examining situations and comparing them with past experiences, while resisting the temptation to respond impulsively, is another of the primary characteristics of smart thinking.

As the child acquires increasing knowledge about himself and about life, he begins to establish his identity, his preferences and his goals. His behaviors, attitudes and choices directly reflect this never-ending filtering, distilling, classifying and filing process. While this is happening, the child is also developing the capacity to discriminate. He selects certain friends, interests and pleasures, and rejects other friends, interests and pleasures. The way he lives his life affirms who he is, what he believes, what he likes, what he wants, how he functions and where he is heading.

The classifying, filing and sorting principles apply to all contexts. The child who fails to activate a "computer search" when faced with an important decision or problem is in danger of becoming the victim of his own poor strategic thinking. If he allows himself to be influenced by another child who has previously led him into trouble, he is signaling that his computer is malfunctioning. Unless he acquires the ability to use his data base of past experiences more effectively, he may have serious difficulty handling life's challenges.

Many children learn how to put related events into categories without formal instruction. For example, a smart child would be able to identify specific actions that upset his parents and produce negative consequences for him. He would realize that certain behaviors invariably trigger negative reactions. These behaviors might include:

★ leaving the kitchen a mess after preparing a snack
★ leaving his bike in the middle of the driveway so that his dad has to get out of the car to move it aside
★ failing to feed the dog
★ leaving his reports to the last minute.

Once the child recognizes that the behaviors will trigger predictable and unpleasant consequences, he is faced with two basic choices:

1. He can continue to do the things that trigger the upset and the negative consequences.
2. He can consciously avoid doing the things that trigger the upset.

The smart child obviously wants to spare himself unnecessary grief. Realizing that his parents' displeasure could stand in the way of him achieving his objectives, he would reject the first option. Smart kids are rarely masochistic!

The child who does not think smart might gravitate toward the first option without necessarily being consciously aware that he is sabotaging himself. Before this pattern can change, the child must be trained to classify information and experiences and identify common denominators. He must expand his level of awareness about what he is doing and about what is happening to him. Once he becomes more conscious of his behavior patterns and his role in creating these patterns, he can begin to exert more constructive control over the events in his life.

The following supplemental activities are designed to provide your child with additional practice in the areas of identifying, classifying and filing life experiences. The goal of the activities is to show your child how to find the threads that link events together and how to use effectively the data stored in his cerebral computer. He can then begin to formulate strategies that will permit him to make positive changes.

Supplemental Acitivty
CLASSIFYING EVENTS
Children ages 7-12

Parent: Let's look at the following events. I'd like to classify them with you and then make up a title for each category. I'll help you with the first set, if you want.

    playing baseball
    writing a report
    preparing for a history exam
    doing math problems
    going to the beach
    mowing the lawn
    making my bed
    receiving a birthday present
    swimming
    receiving a compliment

      feeling happy
      feeling sad
      getting a hug from Mom
      building a model airplane
      riding a bike
      studying spelling words
      feeding the dog
      playing a video game
      taking out the trash
      feeling proud
      getting a raise in allowance

Parent: The first step is to figure how the events are linked. Let's start by putting them in columns that stand for each category. As we group each event, we'll discuss the reasons for putting them in a particular category and we'll choose a name that best describes each category (i.e., School, Fun Activities, Good Feelings, Chores). [Parent initially helps child with process and then lets child complete list. Choices should be discussed.]

CATEGORY	*CATEGORY*	*CATEGORY*	*CATEGORY*
SCHOOL	FUN ACTIVITIES	CHORES	GOOD FEELINGS
writing a report	playing baseball	mowing the lawn	receiving a birthday present

Parent: Now you do the next one on your own. After you're done, we'll discuss your reasons for putting the events in each category and the reason why you chose the title for the category. [You may want to help your child label the categories (i.e., School, Fun Activities, Punishments, Accomplishments) if he is having difficulty.]

> getting an A on a spelling test
> being grounded
> going swimming
> having an argument with your friend
> being sent to your room for misbehavior
> winning an award in soccer
> going to a birthday party
> being punished by the teacher for talking in class
> going skiing
> becoming a starter on the school volleyball team
> having the teacher submit your essay in a contest
> being punished for hitting your sister
> making the honor roll
> seeing a movie

CATEGORY	*CATEGORY*	*CATEGORY*	*CATEGORY*
_____	_____	_____	_____
_____	_____	_____	_____
_____	_____	_____	_____
_____	_____	_____	_____
_____	_____	_____	_____
_____	_____	_____	_____
_____	_____	_____	_____

Supplemental Activity
CLASSIFYING EVENTS
Teenagers ages 13-17

Parent: Below is a list of events. I'd like you to group them into categories. Afterward, we'll discuss your reasons for putting the events in each particular category. If you want, I'll work on the first set with you.

going skiing
proofreading a report
flirting
doing research for a history report
feeling upset because of being grounded
organizing my notebook
arguing with a friend
playing volleyball
feeling bored
reviewing notes
having my feelings hurt
drawing a picture
studying for a midterm exam
shooting baskets with friends
yelling at my brother
feeling rejected
dancing
feeling jealous
planning a study schedule
disagreeing with a parent
going snorkeling
feeling resentful
studying with a friend

CATEGORY	CATEGORY	CATEGORY	CATEGORY
SCHOOL	SPORTS	CONFLICT	FEELINGS
reviewing	going	arguing	feeling
notes	skiing	with a	rejected
		friend	

Parent: Now do the following set on your own.

      buying a schedule and an assignment organizer
      receiving an A- on a report
      planning a picnic at the park
      arguing with friends about what movie to go to
      being given a lead role in the school play
      not being invited to a party
      being asked to write an article for the school
         newspaper
      deciding not to continue a friendship
      feeling proud about having written a good poem
      organizing the school dance
      feeling betrayed by someone
      understanding a difficult equation in algebra class
      making the honor roll
      organizing a coed softball team

CATEGORY	CATEGORY	CATEGORY	CATEGORY
____	____	____	____
____	____	____	____
____	____	____	____
____	____	____	____
____	____	____	____
____	____	____	____
____	____	____	____
____	____	____	____
____	____	____	____

ESTABLISHING DISTANCE

The child who becomes too emotionally entangled in solving a problem is often unable to think smart. As anxiety, stress and frustration mount, the child may begin to lose a clear perspective on the issues, and his efforts may become increasingly counterproductive. Overwhelmed and discouraged, he steps on the accelerator, but he succeeds only in causing his wheels to spin like tires on an icy road.

The smart child who is stymied usually realizes that he must intentionally establish distance from the problem. Recognizing that his resources are stretched to the limit and that he has begun to work at cross-purposes in achieving his objective, he wisely puts the project aside. This temporary disengagement allows him to recharge his physical, emotional and intellectual batteries. As he siphons off counterproductive tension, he develops a fresh perspective and new insights.

When a child steps back and calmly assesses a challenging situation, he is allowing his conscious *and* his unconscious mind to mull over the situation. Innovative strategies and tactics can frequently emerge from this simmering intellectual cauldron that previously might not have appeared possible.

194

The child who knows when to disengage himself has a distinct advantage over the child who flails away at his problems. This same principle operates when someone goes to sleep at night with a seemingly insurmountable problem and awakes in the morning with a solution. By leaving the switch on, the child permits his brain to continue processing, even when it is in repose.

Intentionally establishing distance when one encounters a snag or when a situation becomes challenging requires wisdom and self-discipline. A child must recognize the danger of allowing himself to become overwhelmed when something is not going right. He must also recognize the value of stepping back to consider what is happening and to develop an effective problem-solving strategy.

All glitches have a source. The smart child understands this and tries to identify the source of the problem so that he can resolve it. For example, a teenager might become frustrated as she attempts to connect the components of a new computer. When she turns the switch, she discovers that the computer doesn't work. If she is smart, she will retrace her steps until she finds the mistake. If she cannot figure out the solution, she will stop, take a break, and if necessary, seek help. The alternative is to become increasingly upset until she reaches the point where she becomes non-functional and possibly damages the computer.

With appropriate guidance, children can learn to disengage themselves when they have become counterproductively entangled in a problem. The following supplemental activities are intended to provide your child with additional practice analyzing, classifying and resolving problems.

You will note that there is a progression in these activities. Initially, your child is asked to analyze the behavior of a hypothetical child. This format permits your child to examine counterproductive behavior with a certain degree of emotional detachment, which makes the process less threatening. Later, your child is encouraged to relate his insights to events in his own life and to look for common denominators that might link his behavior with those of the hypothetical child. This progression from a detached, objective assessment to a more personal one avoids the scripted classic parent-child "you should do this" confrontations that often defeat meaningful changes in attitude or performance. The progression also models how distance from a difficult problem usually increases the probability that the problem can be resolved.

Supplemental Activity
ANALYZING A SITUATION
Children ages 7-12

Parent: I'd like to read a story to you, and then I'd like to discuss it with you.

It's 3:15 on Monday afternoon. The back door slams, and Drew drops his books on the floor in the hall. Within 60 seconds, the sixth grader has the refrigerator door open, the milk poured, and two cookies in his hand. Drew then heads for the den where he settles into a comfortable chair and spends the rest of his afternoon watching cartoons and sit-coms. After dinner, the 12-year-old spends 25 minutes on his homework, but not before his parents have had to remind him several times to do so. He writes his book report in 15 minutes. As usual, the report is sloppy and full of spelling and grammar errors. Although Drew understands math, he makes careless mistakes because he does not take the time to check his work. He is also careless about other things and always tries to put off doing his chores. Every day his parents must remind him at least three times to feed the dog. His room is a disaster zone. His parents are frustrated and upset. Convinced that their son lacks common sense, they punish Drew by taking away his bike or sending him to his room, but nothing seems to work.

Parent: I'd like you to pretend that you are Drew's parent. Tell me how you would feel about your son's behavior. Let's list what might concern you as Drew's parent.

_____

_____

_____

_____

_____

Parent: If you feel that Drew has a problem, it would be interesting to

196

analyze what's going on. We'll use the DIBS System you've already learned.

STEP 1: DEFINE the problem in your own words. I'll be the secretary and write down what you think Drew's problem is.

_____

_____

_____

_____

_____

STEP 2: INVESTIGATE the issues. For example, do you feel that Drew's room is too messy? Do you think a sixth-grader should be expected to keep his room neat? Let's write down your thoughts.

_____

_____

_____

_____

_____

STEP 3: BRAINSTORM a solution. What could you suggest that might help Drew change his behavior? Suggest changes that you feel Drew would agree to make.

_____

_____

_____

_____

197

What do you think Drew's objections might be to these suggestions? Do you think that you could convince him to make the changes? If he refused, what could you, as Drew's parent, do? Let's list your ideas.

_____

_____

_____

_____

_____

Do you feel that you do any of the things that Drew does? If the answer to the question is "yes," let's do the next step.

STEP 4: *SELECT an idea* produced by brainstorming that Drew or you might test. For example, what steps could you take to make changes in your behavior? Let's list them.

_____

_____

_____

_____

_____

Supplemental Activity
ANALYZING A SITUATION
Teenagers ages 13-17

Parent: I'd like to read something to you and I'd like your reactions.

It's 5:00 on Monday afternoon and Ashley has just gotten home after volleyball practice. As soon as she enters the house, the

198

16-year-old heads for the telephone. She has important things to discuss with her best friend Marci and spends the next 22 minutes talking with her. When her call is complete, she begins her homework and works for a half hour before dinner. After dinner, Ashley spends 45 minutes talking with her other friends. Her remaining homework is sandwiched between telephone calls, and is more or less completed by 8:15. By 8:20, she is again on the phone. When her calling is finally completed at 9:00, she begins watching television and does so until bedtime at 10:30. In Spanish class the next morning, Ashley discovers that she has forgotten to study for the quiz that her teacher announced the previous day. Because of her natural ability in foreign languages and her excellent memory skills, she somehow manages to get a C- on the quiz. That evening Ashley decides to put off the library research for her science report until the weekend. The eight-page report is due Monday morning.

If you were Ashley's parents, would you be concerned? If so, could you tell me what things might disturb you? Let's write them down.

_____

_____

_____

_____

Parent: Let's operate on the assumption that you feel that Ashley does have a problem. We'll use the DIBS System you've already learned for the problem analysis.

STEP 1: DEFINE the problem in your own words. I'll be the secretary and write it down.

_____

_____

_____

_____

_____

STEP 2: *INVESTIGATE the issues.* For example, you might feel that Ashley is not spending enough time studying. Or, do you think a high school junior should limit the amount of time spent on the phone? Let's write down your thoughts.

— _____

_____

_____

_____

_____

_____

STEP 3: *BRAINSTORM a solution.* In other words, what would you suggest to improve the situation?

_____

_____

_____

_____

_____

Parent: Do you think that Ashley would agree to these changes? If she didn't, what could you do? Let's list her parents' options:

200

_____ _____

_____ _____

_____ _____

_____

_____

Parent: Do you feel that you have any of the same traits that Ashley does? If the answer is "yes," let's do Step 4.

STEP 4: SELECT an idea that Ashley might test. For example, in view of what you concluded about Ashley, what steps might _you_ take to make some positive changes? Let's list them.

_____

_____

_____

_____

_____

LEARNING HOW TO NEGOTIATE

No child can escape occasionally being in conflict or disagreement with someone else. The person on the other side of the issue might be a parent, a friend, a brother, a sister or a teacher. When confronted with a conflict, a child is faced with five possible outcomes:

1. He can submit to the will of the other person.
2. He can defeat or neutralize his "adversary."
3. He can go around the other person.
4. He can create a standoff.
5. He can negotiate with the other person.

Although conflicts of interest are inevitable, these disagreements do not have to lead to a battle. Smart people realize that they have an alternative: they can negotiate a settlement.

Producing a mutually acceptable compromise requires that those in disagreement be willing to discard the traditional "winner/loser" mind-set. Each party must be prepared to evaluate his respective position and make concessions.

Although the smart child likes to win when forced by circumstances to fight, he is astute enough to recognize that avoiding unnecessary battles makes sense. Being strategic, he realizes that conflicts, hurt feelings and resentment can erect major barriers to him achieving his defined objectives. Having trained himself to think analytically and rationally, he recognizes the value of negotiating a reasonable compromise whenever possible. Nevertheless, the smart child is not necessarily willing to compromise on all issues. He knows the limits, and he realizes the importance of protecting himself and his reputation. His ingrained appreciation of cause and effect permits him to recognize when he would endanger himself by agreeing to unwise compromises. Such matters as cheating, stealing or lying would be non-negotiable. If a friend, for example, were to attempt to encourage him to cheat or steal or to help someone else cheat or steal, the smart child would say "no."

The ability to resolve conflicts is one of the ultimate acid tests of a child's problem-solving skills. This capacity is especially important when a child finds himself in conflict with his parents. Most parent-child disagreements involve limit-setting. They usually develop when parents assert their prerogative to establish rules, guidelines and standards, and when their children attempt to bend or modify these rules, guidelines and standards.

In some situations, family rules may be bent without undermining the parents' prerogatives or authority. This is especially true when a child can present a plausible justification for parents to re-examine their position. Certain limits, however, are clearly non-negotiable.

For instance, parents would undoubtedly refuse to serve liquor at a party held in their home after the senior prom. The teenager may disagree and may present what he considers to be reasonable arguments for serving beer to his friends. Obviously, this issue would be non-negotiable. The family rule is clear, unequivocal and reasonable: No liquor will be served to teenagers in this home, period. Although the parents should be willing to explain their reasons, they need not feel any obligation to budge from their position.

Not every situation is as black and white as the issue of serving liquor to minors. The line separating non-negotiable family laws and negotiable issues can sometimes be obscure. For example, a child who has a specified bedtime may be able to present a persuasive rationale for staying up on a particular night to see a special program. The child's parents would have to decide whether the child's reasons justify reconsidering the child's bedtime on that particular evening.

Although there can be special circumstances that might justify modifying family rules, having certain rules that are non-negotiable serves a vital psychological and character-forming function during the formative years of a child's life. The child who concludes that every family rule is subject to bargaining can easily become confused and insecure. Once he considers bedtime, mealtime and family responsibilities as subject to haggling, he may begin to perceive life as one big swap meet. Such a child is a high-risk candidate for becoming manipulative.

Clearly defined family structure and guidelines provide a child with an important sense of security. The child who is raised in a family system in which the rules are poorly defined may spend his entire life trying to determine what the limits are. Because he has not internalized a sense of structure and order and a clearly defined value system, he may feel compelled to test society's rules. Such a child could get into serious trouble.

The child who is confused because his parents have not defined the guidelines and standards frequently evolves into a confused adult. In his desire to define the dos and don'ts, he may be attracted to alternative belief systems or even to cults that seem to provide the answers that were lacking during his childhood.

Parents are faced with a crucial dilemma: when should they negotiate with their child (and thus teach their child how to negotiate), and when should they refuse to negotiate? Although children must be taught that all issues cannot be negotiated, they must also be taught how to become effective negotiators if they are to survive and prevail in a competitive world.

The smart child realizes that by negotiating, she can avoid knock-down fights, impasses and defeats. In contrast, the not-so-smart child often feels compelled either to assault every potential adversary or to avoid every potential conflict. Such a child could begin to perceive life as a continual battleground or a never-ending detour.

One of the basic lessons that a child must learn about negotiation is that a settlement is far easier to achieve when everyone feels they have won something. The smart child realizes that a mutually advantageous resolution of conflict reduces resentment and establishes a positive, problem-solving context for the resolution of future conflicts.

203

You should be able to identify specific areas of recurring disagreement with your child that might lend themselves to negotiation. These issues should be carefully selected so that your child does not become confused about the family's position on other non-negotiable issues. For example, let's assume that your child asks to stay up late on a particular evening to watch a special TV program. The situation clearly presents a potential conflict of interest and a potential opportunity for reaching a mutually acceptable settlement. If a conflict develops over the issue, there are four possible outcomes:

Parent	Child
1. Wins (bedtime enforced)	Loses (forced to concede)
2. Loses (concedes)	Wins (extends bedtime)
3. Loses (argument/upset)	Loses (argument/upset)
4. Wins (negotiated compromise)	Wins (negotiated compromise)

Let's examine four hypothetical dialogues that might produce these four different outcomes.

Scenario #1

Child: Can I stay up till 9:30 to see the gymnastics competition?
Parent: I'm sorry honey, it's past your bedtime.
Child: But the Olympics only happen every 4 years! And I want to be in the Olympics someday.
Parent: No. Bedtime is at 9:00. You know the rule.

Scenario #2

Child: Can I stay up till 9:30 to see the gymnastics competition?
Parent: You know, you keep finding reasons to stay up past your bedtime, and Mom and I are getting concerned. We'll allow you to stay up, but this has got to stop.

Scenario #3

Child: Can I stay up till 9:30 to see the gymnastics competition?
Parent: You're always trying to con us into letting you stay up beyond your bedtime. The answer is "no." Period and end of discussion.

| Child: | You never give me a chance to explain anything. You just say no, no, no! |

Scenario #4

Child:	Can I stay up till 9:30 to see the gymnastics competition?
Parent:	Well, that poses a problem. We feel it's important that you get to bed at a reasonable hour so that you can do well in school the next day. Dad and I also feel that there are rules that should be kept. If we let you stay up whenever something interesting is on TV, then the bedtime rule no longer exists. Do you see the danger in this?
Child:	Yeah, I guess. But I won't do it again. Just tonight. I want to be a gymnast in the Olympics too, and I want to see this program.
Parent:	Let's look at some possible solutions. We could call your uncle and ask him if he could videotape the program. Then you could go over there tomorrow and see it. If he's not home, we'll compromise. We'll let you stay up till 9:30 tonight, but in the future you'll have to make your own arrangements to have programs videotaped in advance. After tonight, the 9:00 bedtime curfew on school nights will be enforced. Agreed?
Child:	OK.

In scenario #1, the parent prevails and gets his way in the negotiation process. This outcome is very common, for parents obviously have more power than their children, especially during the early stages of childhood. Although parents may choose to be firm about family rules, they should be willing to explain to their child why they feel they cannot make exceptions to the rule. They might examine the importance of being alert in school the next day. It is possible that despite his parents' explanations, the child might feel he is being treated unfairly, and he may become angry or resentful. Children handle hostility in different ways. One child may repress his feelings. The emotions will implode and cause the child to become discouraged and demoralized. Another child may express the feelings by acting out. In either event, the child's self-esteem could be jeopardized, especially if he continually loses these conflicts of interest with his parents.

Unfortunately, some parents reject their child's position without examining the issues. Usually such parents defend their response by arguing that a rule is a rule. Although inflexibility about rules might be justified when parents are convinced that their child is a chronic rule-bender, it can have very damaging implications if the child does not have a history of being manipulative. The parent's reaction sends a clear message to the child: "Your insights and position have no credibility."

The child whose arguments are rejected without due process is at risk for developing negative associations about his ability to negotiate conflicts of interest. Although he may decide to use a more persuasive argument the next time he presents his case, it is more likely that he will simply conclude that negotiation with his parents is impossible. He may manifest his anger by "getting back" in direct or indirect ways. He may become disobedient and purposely do things to make his parents angry, or he may become passively resistant and break the rules slyly or secretly.

Another possibility is that the child might conclude that he lacks the ability to negotiate. This conclusion could plague him throughout his life. As an adult, he may need to enter into important negotiations for the sale of a home or he may need to negotiate a contract. If he has imprinted negative associations with his ability to negotiate, he will be at an economic and psychological disadvantage. The development of the child's self-confidence and self-esteem cannot help but be affected by negative childhood experiences.

Although it would probably require more than simply one bad experience to undermine a child's confidence in his ability to negotiate, a series of negative experiences during the formative years could easily undermine the child's self-confidence. If the child is forced to lose repeatedly simply because he has less power than his parents, he might decide that he is intrinsically powerless.

Some parents may consider an issue such as bedtime non-negotiable. Indeed, this should probably be the case with younger children. However, there may be exceptional and justifiable reasons why a child might want to extend his bedtime temporarily or permanently. For example, a 12-year-old may be convinced that she does not need as much sleep as a 10-year-old, and she may be justified in feeling this way. Before categorically rejecting her position, her parents might propose an experiment to determine how much sleep she requires, or they might consult with her pediatrician. Should the child be able to demonstrate that she can indeed function well with less sleep, her position should be considered. The alternative is to reject her attempts to negotiate, and in the process, deny her an opportunity to learn how to negotiate.

206

In scenario #2, the parent loses and the child wins. If the child is a chronic rule-bender, the parent's response clearly signals that he has "bought into" his son's manipulative behavior. This same behavior probably manifests itself in other areas of the child's life. For instance, the child may have decided to deliver newspapers in the afternoon. After doing this for several days, he realizes that the job requires more work than he planned. To save time, he tries to persuade his mother to drive him along his route so that he can throw the papers out of the back of the car. If the parent agrees to this arrangement, she has communicated that her son can expect to be rescued every time he confronts a challenge. From this the child would most likely conclude that he is not responsible for his decisions and his actions. Although he may feel that he has won because he got what he wanted, it is clear that he has actually lost. Settlements predicated on manipulation are in no one's best interest.

In scenario #3, both parties lose because the conflict of interests has deteriorated into a bitter argument. The parent sacrifices an important opportunity to deal with the issue of responsibility, and the child psychologically imprints that he cannot negotiate effectively with his parents. The family communication system is clearly predicated on power, distrust and resentment.

In scenario #4, both parties win. The parent uses the situation as an opportunity to communicate with the child about the issue of family rules and to brainstorm a possible solution to the immediate problem. If this solution proves unfeasible (i.e., the uncle is not home), she agrees to an alternative compromise, but only in this instance. She serves notice that she is not establishing a precedent about the bedtime rule. Although she is willing to bend the rule this time, she clearly communicates that he will have to make alternative arrangements if the situation should recur.

Knowing when to negotiate with your child demands a judgment call. There are no firm guidelines. By helping your child appreciate that there are situations that lend themselves to negotiation and by helping him appreciate which situations fall into the negotiable category, you are modeling how the smart-thinking process can be applied to real life situations.

"I KNOW I'M SMART!"

The child who can make this statement has acquired formidable power. His words testify to his faith in his ability to take charge of his life and make things happen according to his own plan.

207

Smartness is a state of mind and a thinking orientation that reflects a child's conviction that he can deal with life effectively. The child *knows* he is smart because he realizes that he has proven to himself that he has the ability to prevail over challenges and problems. This positive track record forms the foundation for the development of self-confidence and self-esteem. Goal-oriented, analytical, responsible and motivated, the smart child has put himself on a winning track and he is committed to staying on that track.

The smart child is like someone who survives a small plane crash in a dense jungle. After extricating himself from the wreckage, he surveys the situation, assesses his resources and develops a plan for getting back to civilization. His confidence in his ability to survive derives not only from his faith in his own power, but also from practical strategic thinking. Before beginning his journey, the pilot was smart enough to pack survival gear in the plane.

Sometimes a child naturally acquires confidence in his own intellectual potency. In most cases, however, the capacity to think efficiently and effectively must be carefully cultivated. Initially, parents and teachers must help the child till the intellectual soil. When he is able and willing, the child can take over.

It matters little whether your child becomes convinced of his smartness naturally or requires your guidance and assistance. What does matter is that your child acquire the conviction that he can figure out how to make his life work.

This book is only the first step in the cultivation process. Do not let the process stop on the last page! Like any skill or talent, smart thinking must be continually practiced and applied, or it will atrophy like an unused muscle. Encourage your child to stretch his limits. Acknowledge and affirm him at each step of the way. Support him when he stumbles. Love him for his uniqueness. The payoff for your efforts will be a child whose mind is active and potent and whose life is full and rewarding.

Chapter 8
Follow-up Inventories

RE-EVALUATING YOUR CHILD

The time has come for you to determine whether or not your efforts—and your child's efforts—have produced a higher Smartness Quotient. The follow-up checklists below will permit you to compare your initial impressions about your child's attitudes, behavior and performance with your current impressions.

You will note that extra columns have been added to the checklists. After you fill in your current impressions, it is recommended that you refer to the initial checklist and record your original reactions in the second set of columns. By inserting your initial impressions *after* you have completed the follow-up checklist, you reduce the chances of being influenced by the first checklist. You can then make a comparison, and if you think it beneficial, you can do additional work with your child in those areas in which he or she might still be deficient.

If you have used the communication strategies in this book and if they have produced positive results, continue to use them! Encouraging your child to think smart and to analyze problems should become an integral strand that is intentionally woven into the family fabric.

Ideally, your child is now thinking smarter. Although it would be wonderful if he shows improvement in all areas, do not be disappointed if there are still some deficit areas. Your expectations should be high, but they should also be realistic. Even if only some of the behaviors and attitudes that were previously undermining your child's performance have been corrected, your efforts have been worthwhile. The door is now open for additional gains.

Although your child may have made dramatic improvement, do not expect him to think smart all the time. Everyone has mental lapses when he does not respond ideally. Your primary objective is to reduce the incidence of these lapses and to orient your child toward using his intelligence effectively. Remind yourself that even a child with a highly developed Smartness Quotient is fallible and will from time to time do some not-so-smart things.

Look for progress. Acknowledge your child when he is thinking smart. Express confidence in his reasoning ability. You can achieve far better results when you intentionally create a positive, supportive environment. Your child wants your approval. He wants to feel that his efforts are appreciated and that an occasional miscue or regression will not trigger a rejection.

The ultimate goal is for your child to integrate smart thinking skills into his daily life. In some situations, he will think smart reflexively. In other situations, he will have to push his smart-thinking button intentionally. You will know that your child has "arrived" when you see him encounter a challenge, stop to analyze the situation and systematically go about resolving the problem. Like the martial arts, smart-thinking skills are a resource that is available when needed. The child who knows how and when to use his problem-solving weapons is all but invincible.

Checklist for Parent
CAUSE AND EFFECT
(Chapter 1—Page 20)

Code. 0 = Never   1 = Rarely
      2 = Sometimes   3 = Often   4 = Always

	Current	Previous
My child leaves projects and assignments until the last minute.	_____	_____
My child does not allow sufficient time to complete projects.	_____	_____
My child is disorganized.	_____	_____
My child acts impulsively and without thinking.	_____	_____

My child is chronically forgetful. _____ _____

My child repeats the same mistakes. _____ _____

My child resists assistance. _____ _____

My child rarely establishes short-term or long-term goals. _____ _____

My child has little sense of purpose. _____ _____

My child gives up easily. _____ _____

My child avoids responsibility. _____ _____

My child tends to blame others for his or her problems. _____ _____

My child is not especially concerned about potential danger or risk. _____ _____

My child appears satisfied to do a second-rate job. _____ _____

Checklist for Parent ATTITUDES
(Chapter 2—Page 43)

Code: 0 = Never   1 = Rarely
     2 = Sometimes   3 = Often   4 = Always

	Current	Previous
My child is willing to take reasonable risks.	_____	_____
My child is enthusiastic about seeking and accepting new challenges.	_____	_____
My child enjoys finding solutions to problems.	_____	_____
My child likes to test and stretch his or her limits.	_____	_____
My child has faith in his or her ability to succeed at whatever he or she undertakes.	_____	_____
My child completes projects.	_____	_____
My child takes pride in doing a first-rate job.	_____	_____

211

My child perseveres despite setbacks. _____ _____

My child feels he or she deserves to "win." _____ _____

My child feels he or she is a valuable _____ _____
person.

My child feels he or she is intelligent. _____ _____

Checklist for Parent
PROBLEM-MANAGEMENT
(Chapter 3—Page 75)

Code: 0 = Never   1 = Rarely
      2 = Sometimes   3 = Often   4 = Always

	Current	Previous
My child tends to avoid confronting problems or challenges.	_____	_____
My child insists on getting his or her own way, even if it is not working.	_____	_____
My child is unwilling to accept suggestions and help.	_____	_____
My child gets upset when frustrated.	_____	_____
My child cannot think clearly when upset or frustrated.	_____	_____
My child gives up easily.	_____	_____
My child has difficulty developing strategies for solving problems.	_____	_____
My child is disorganized.	_____	_____
My child tends to blame others for his or her problems.	_____	_____
My child is passive.	_____	_____
My child easily accepts that problems are insurmountable.	_____	_____
My child tends to repeat the same mistakes.	_____	_____
My child becomes defensive when a	_____	_____

problem is pointed out.

My child procrastinates when faced with a challenge, problem or chore.   _____ _____

My child denies that he or she has problems that must be resolved.   _____ _____

TOTAL   _____ _____

Checklist for Parent
GOALS
(Chapter 4—Page 97)

Code: 0 = Never   1 = Rarely
      2 = Sometimes   3 = Often   4 = Always

	Current	Previous
My child defines specific objectives.		
My child's goals are realistic.		
My child takes the time to plan ahead.		
My child is able to establish priorities.		
My child is able to budget and manage time effectively.		
My child can develop a workable plan for attaining his or her objectives.		
My child establishes interim goals.		
My child is willing to suspend immediate gratification in order to attain his or her goals.		
My child bounces back from setbacks.		
My child can handle frustration.		
My child persists despite encountering difficulty.		
My child likes challenges and likes to test himself or herself		
My child believes he or she can prevail.		

My child is proud of his or her
accomplishments. _____ _____

My child establishes a new goal once he or
she attains a particular objective. _____ _____

TOTAL _____ _____

Checklist for Parent
TIME-MANAGEMENT
(Chapter 5—Page 136)

Code: 0 = Never   1 = Rarely
2 = Sometimes   3 = Often   4 = Always

	Current	Previous
My child leaves projects and assignments to the last minute.	_____	_____
My child doesn't seem to care about getting things done on time.	_____	_____
My child does not have a schedule.	_____	_____
My child hands in material that is inaccurate and sloppy.	_____	_____
My child often hands in assignments that are incomplete.	_____	_____
My child does not hand in assignments.	_____	_____
My child has difficulty estimating accurately how much time a project will require.	_____	_____
My child lacks planning skills.	_____	_____
My child is often under stress caused by poor time-management.	_____	_____
My child does not consider the time required to perform the interim steps necessary for achieving an objective.	_____	_____
My child schedules too many things to do at one time.	_____	_____
My child does not leave enough time for	_____	_____

reviewing and proofing his assignments.

My child is late for appointments. _____ _____

My child's time-management behaviors create stress in the family. _____ _____

TOTAL _____ _____

Checklist for Parent
LEARNING FROM MISTAKES
(Chapter 6—Page 160)

Code: 0 = Never 1 = Rarely
          2 = Sometimes 3 = Often 4 = Always

	Current	Previous
My child become discouraged when he or she makes a mistake.	_____	_____
My child is afraid of making mistakes.	_____	_____
My child tends to give up if he or she makes a mistake.	_____	_____
My child makes the same mistake repeatedly.	_____	_____
My child fails to examine his or her mistakes.	_____	_____
My child does not perceive the common denominators that characterize his or her mistakes.	_____	_____
My child does not admit that he or she has made a mistake.	_____	_____
My child's judgment is deficient.	_____	_____
My child is defensive about mistakes.	_____	_____
My child is unwilling to discuss mistakes with me.	_____	_____
My child blames others for his mistakes.	_____	_____
TOTAL	_____	_____

Checklist for Parent
BOUNCING BACK FROM SETBACKS
(Chapter 6—Page 167)

Code: 0 = Never   1 = Rarely
    2 = Sometimes   3 = Often   4 = Always

	Current	Previous
My child gets very discouraged when he suffers a setback.	_____	_____
My child is tempted to give up when he fails at something.	_____	_____
My child tries to avoid things that are difficult.	_____	_____
My child is convinced he is dumb when he has a setback.	_____	_____
My child regrets having tried something when he has not done well.	_____	_____
My child believes people think less of him if they know he has failed at something.	_____	_____
My child doesn't like to admit that he has had a setback.	_____	_____
My child wants to run away and hide after a failure.	_____	_____
When my child is doing something that becomes too difficult, he quits.	_____	_____
My child is unwilling to ask for help.	_____	_____
When my child encounters difficulty, he gets so frustrated that he can no longer work efficiently.	_____	_____
If my child is forced to ask for help, he becomes defensive.	_____	_____
TOTAL	_____	_____

HAVING YOUR CHILD RE-EVALUATE HIMSELF OR HERSELF

The follow-up inventories found below are not intended to be a "final exam," but are intended to offer your child an opportunity to gauge changes in behavior and attitude. They should be presented positively, and your child should be assured that there will be no negative consequences if problem areas still exist. If your child feels he should answer in a certain way in order to please you, he will not respond forthrightly to the statements. Do not record your child's previous responses until *after* he has completed the current checklist.

You might want to present the follow-up checklists in the following way: "As we worked together on this book, you were asked to complete certain checklists which gave information about your problem-solving attitudes and behaviors. Do you remember that I told you that you would be asked to complete the same checklists at the end of the book. Well, the time has now come to do so. I'd like you to respond to the statements, and then we'll compare your current responses to your previous ones. This is not a test. The follow-up checklists will simply help us determine what changes have occurred. We can look at the changes, and we can also look at the areas in which there have been no changes. When you are done with each checklist, we'll go back and record your original response."

Checklist for Child
ATTITUDES
(Chapter 2—Page 50)

Code: 0 = Never   1 = Rarely
         2 = Sometimes   3 = Often   4 = Always

	Current	Previous
I like challenges.		
It's important that I do well in school.		
I enjoy finding and correcting my mistakes.		
I believe that I can do a good job if I want to.		
I can do good work even if I am not very excited about the project.		

217

I like to test myself to find out how good I am. _____ _____

I can handle setbacks. _____ _____

I learn from mistakes and try not to make the same mistakes again. _____ _____

I am willing to accept help when I am stuck or confused. _____ _____

I believe that my friends respect me. _____ _____

I believe that my teachers respect me. _____ _____

I believe that my parents respect me. _____ _____

People think that I am a hard worker. _____ _____

I like school. _____ _____

I think I am smart. _____ _____

I finish projects that I start. _____ _____

I enjoy getting good grades. _____ _____

I enjoy developing my skills and talents. _____ _____

I enjoy finding solutions to problems. _____ _____

I am not afraid to take a risk and try something difficult. _____ _____

TOTAL _____ _____

Checklist for Child
MANAGING PROBLEMS
(Chapter 3—Page 77)

Code: 0 = Never   1 = Rarely
        2 = Sometimes   3 = Often   4 = Always

	Current	Previous
I avoid trying to solve problems.	_____	_____
I insist on getting my own way, even if it is not working.	_____	_____
I am not willing to accept suggestions and help.	_____	_____

I get upset when I become frustrated. ____ ____

I have difficulty doing something when I am upset or frustrated. ____ ____

I give up when a job is difficult. ____ ____

I have difficulty figuring out how to solve problems. ____ ____

I do not have the materials I need to do the job. ____ ____

I blame others for my problems. ____ ____

I make the same mistakes over and over. ____ ____

I don't like it when someone points out a problem. ____ ____

I tend to put off dealing with problems or chores. ____ ____

I don't like to admit that there is a problem or challenge that I need to deal with. ____ ____

TOTAL ____ ____

Checklist for Child
GOALS
(Chapter 4—Page 98)

Code: 0 = Never   1 = Rarely
2 = Sometimes   3 = Often   4 = Always

	Current	Previous
I have goals that I want to achieve.		
My goals are realistic.		
I establish specific objectives. For example, I know what grade I would like to get in each of my courses.		
I feel that I have the ability to get what I want.		
I figure out a plan for reaching my long-term goals.		

When I have a project or assignment to do, I decide what steps I must go through in order to reach my goal.

I am able to schedule my time so that I can get my work done.

I am able to establish priorities (what's most important).

I am patient as I work toward reaching my goals.

I enjoy learning new skills.

I enjoy improving my skills.

I am willing to continue working hard even if I have a problem or a setback.

I am willing to continue working hard even if I become frustrated or upset.

I like challenges.

I feel good when I overcome a challenge or a problem.

When I achieve my goal, I feel proud.

I like to set a new goal for myself after I achieve a particular goal.

TOTAL

Checklist for Child
TIME-MANAGEMENT
(Chapter 5—Page 137)

Code: 0 = Never   1 = Rarely
     2 = Sometimes   3 = Often   4 = Always

	Current	Previous
I leave my projects and assignments to the last minute.		
The work I hand in has errors.		
I do not hand in assignments on time.		

220

My work is sloppy.   _____   _____

I get upset because I don't have enough   _____   _____
time.

My work is incomplete.   _____   _____

My work is handed in late.   _____   _____

I have difficulty planning how much time I   _____   _____
need to complete a project.

I schedule too many things to do at one   _____   _____
time.

I do not leave enough time to check over   _____   _____
my work.

I am late for school, appointments or   _____   _____
meetings.

I don't use a schedule.   _____   _____

TOTAL   _____   _____

Checklist for Child
LEARNING FROM MISTAKES
(Chapter 6—Page 161)

Code: 0 = Never   1 = Rarely
     2 = Sometimes   3 = Often   4 = Always

	Current	Previous
I get discouraged when I make a mistake.	_____	_____
I am afraid of making a mistake.	_____	_____
I tend to give up when I make a mistake.	_____	_____
I tend to make the same mistake over and over again.	_____	_____
I don't take the time to examine why I make mistakes.	_____	_____
I don't look for the common denominators that link my mistakes. (Explain.)	_____	_____
I don't like to admit that I've made a	_____	_____

mistake.

I don't think carefully about what I am doing. _____ _____

I become defensive when I make a mistake. _____ _____
(Explain.)

I don't like to discuss my mistakes with my _____ _____
parents or teachers.

I tend to blame others for my mistakes. _____ _____

TOTAL _____ _____

Checklist for Child
SETBACKS
(Chapter 6—Page 169)

Code: 0 = Never   1 = Rarely
     2 = Sometimes   3 = Often   4 = Always

	Current	Previous
I get very discouraged when I have a setback.	_____	_____
I feel like giving up when I fail at something.	_____	_____
I try to avoid doing something that is difficult for me.	_____	_____
I feel dumb when I have a setback.	_____	_____
I regret having tried something when I did not do well.	_____	_____
I think people think less of me if they know I have failed at something.	_____	_____
I don't like to admit that I have had a setback.	_____	_____
I want to run away and hide after a failure.	_____	_____
If I am doing something and it gets too difficult, I quit.	_____	_____

I don't like to ask for help.   _____   _____

When I encounter difficulty I get so   _____   _____
frustrated that I can no longer work
efficiently.

If I have to ask for help, I feel stupid.   _____   _____

TOTAL   _____   _____

A MESSAGE TO KIDS

Being smart means that you have a special passport. This passport is like a free VIP (Very Important Person) pass to Disneyland that allows you to see everything in the park, avoid long lines and take unlimited rides.

Your passport lets everybody know that you are special and that you can solve problems, establish goals, and do a first-rate job. It tells the world that you know how to think.

You can choose to use your passport to get good grades, or you can use it to convince your parents that you are mature and responsible and deserve more freedom. You can even use it to develop a plan to get the most out of your basketball skills or your math skills.

Remind yourself to use your passport whenever you are faced with a challenge. Like an athlete, you must continually train yourself so that your skills stay sharp. You must ask questions. You must look at what is happening in the world around you. Are you doing your best work in school? Are you getting along with your parents? You must also examine what is happening to the feelings within you. Are you upset? Are you confused?

Everyone occasionally faces problems and challenges in life. You are no exception. Unlike kids who don't think smart, _you_ have an important advantage. You already know how to solve many of the problems you will face. Being smart, you also know that you can seek help when you can't solve a problem alone.

Developing smart-thinking skills is like developing strong, hard muscles. If you don't keep exercising, your muscles will get soft. It's the same with thinking. Once you stop using your smart-thinking skills, your brain can also become "soft."

Don't let your passport expire. Practice what you have learned in this book. You now have a special talent. You're much too smart to waste it!

Index

A

Ability, natural 36
Ability, potential 12
Accomplishments 34
Achievement 36
Achievement loop 101
Achievement potential 3
Acid test 187
Acknowledgment 69
Acting irresponsibly 27
Active involvement 26
Active learning 4
Active listening 16
Active participation 42, 102, 113
Admonishments 102
Affirmation 165
Aggressiveness 68
"Ain't I wonderful" role 173
Alienation 2
Alternative strategy approach 175
Alternatives 44
Analogies 45, 48, 173
Analysis, problem 8
Analysis, process of 159
Analytical process 8
Analytical-thinking skills 4, 7, 183
Analyzing 36
Anger 67
Answers, non-logical 27
Anxiety 175
Applying Intelligence 32-63
Aptitude 12, 35
Arguments 2
Arguments, persuasive 206
Assessment, objective 195
Associations, negative 34, 177
Attitudes 44, 48
Authority, parents' 202
Autocratic approach 112
Aversion 34
Avoidance behavior 37, 40
Awareness, lack of 68

B

Balance, emotional 125
Barriers 33

Barriers, psychological 177
Basics 15
Behavior modification 68
Behavior, avoidance 37
Behavior, defeating 133
Behavior, non-adaptive 67
Behavior, phobic 37
Behavior, protective 34
Behavior, reactionary 139
Behavioral goals 16
Blaming 102
Bounce Back, Learning to 156-179
Bounce-back quotient 168
Brainstorming 27
Breakdowns, communication 2
Bypassing 36

C

Camouflaging 40
Capableness 36
Career decisions 104
Cause and effect 15
Cerebral "turbocharger" 183
Cerebral shutdown 159
Challenges 75, 157
Character 117
Cheating 102
Checking the hypothesis 10
Checklist, problem-management 75
Childhood experiences,
    negative 206
Choices 70
Chores 105
"Circle the wagons" 176
Classifying events 189
Classifying principles 188
Coaching 39
Collecting data 10
Common denominators 159
Communication 5
Communication breakdowns 2
Communication "delivery
    system" 102
Communication strategies 5, 15
Compensation 39, 40
Compensatory systems 40

Competence 36
Competency 45
Compromise 202
Conclusions 42
Conduct 42
Conflicts of interest 202
Conflicts, resolving 202
Confused adults 203
Consequences 15
Control 41
Cooperation 42, 102, 136
Counseling 132
Counterproductive attitudes 44
Creativity 23
Credibility 161, 206
Critical thinking 4, 15
Crossroads 65
Curiosity 4
Cycles 70

D
Data base 187
Data collection 10
Decision-making, strategic 61
Decisions, career 104
Decisions, flawed 1
Deductive 157
Defeating behavior 133
Defense mechanisms 34, 131
Defensive wall 103
Defensiveness 42
Deficiencies 34, 39
Deficiencies in reasoning 27
Deficient skills 12
Deficits 34
Delinquency 102
Democratic approach 112
Demoralization 170
Denial 41
Dependency 133, 134
Deserving to prevail 157
Desperation 133
Developing the Capacity to
     Think 7-31
Development, intellectual 11
Developmental stages 11

DIBS system 49
Dilemmas 75
Diligence 102, 132
Disagreements, parent-child 202
Disapproval 101
Discipline, self- 102
Discouragement 101
Disharmony 131
Disinterest 130
Disorganization 34, 134
Disorientation 34
Distortions in perception 177
Drugs 102

E
Education 12
Efficient thought 12
Effort 45, 102
Egoism 104, 157
Emotional balance 125
Emotional energy 34, 37
Emotional vulnerability 27
Empathy 42
Encouragement 35, 69
Energy 34, 118
Environment, home 117
Environmental chaos 147
Errors 159
Establishing distance 194
Establishing goals 4
Establishing priorities 4
Establishing Priorities and
     Goals 94-128
Ethical issues 26, 90
Events, classifying 189
Examination process 27
Examination/alternative strategy
     approach 175
Excessive nurturing 134
Excuses 131
Expectations 39, 132
Expectations, negative 159
Expectations, parent's 132
Experiences, negative 34, 206
External order 148
External structure 148

F

Facility 35
Family influences 13, 131
Family laws, non-negotiable 202
Family tension 131
Fear 41, 176
Feedback 68
Feelings 42
Filing principles 188
Financial survival 41
Flawed decisions 1
Focused intelligence 19
Focusing 10, 118
Follow-up Inventories 209-223
Forbearance 42
Forgetfulness 34, 102
Formal education 12
Formative years 34
Fragmented families 13
Frontal assaults 42
Frustration 2
Fuel injectors 70

G

General intelligence 37
Genetics 3
Glitches 195
Goal-abandonment 121
Goal-directed child 94
Goal-directed effort 12
Goal-fixated child 125
Goals and achievements, periodic
    review 121
Goals and priorities 94-128
Goals and problem-solving 4
Goals, behavioral 16
Goals, establishing 4
Goals, inappropriate 115
Goals, long-term 104, 114
Goals, medium-range 114
Goals, short-term 114
Good judgment 187
Ground rules 144
Guidance 11
Guidelines 15, 38, 132

H

Habits, self-defeating 131
Helplessness drama 134
Hierarchy 106
Home environment 117
Honesty 22
Human potential 68
Hypothesis, checking the 10

I

IQ 8
IQ test 37
Identifying 36
Identifying important information 4
Identity 34
Impasses 203
Imprinting 34, 177
Inadequacies 34, 176
Inappropriate goals 115
Incentives 69
Incompetence 34, 39, 40
Inefficient use of time 133
Inflexibility 206
Influences, family 131
Information, identifying important 4
Information, remembering 4
Inhibitions 148, 170
Innermost feelings 176
Inquisitiveness 157
Insecurities 27, 39, 41
Insight 70
Instincts 39
Instruction 39, 35
Intellectual curiosity 4
Intellectual development 11
Intellectual energies 37
Intellectual limitations 39
Intellectual potency 208
Intellectual resourses 11
Intelligence, focused 19
Intelligence, general 9, 10, 37
Interacting 4
Internal structure 148
Internalizing 45
Interpretations 42
Intervention 136

Introduction 1-6
Introspection 26, 70
Introspection, purposeful 71
Introspection, strategic 64-93
Intuition 40
Inventories, follow-up 209-223
Irresponsibility 27, 102, 118
Issues, ethical 26
Issues, negotiable 202-203
Issues, underlying 27

J
Judgment 187
Judgment calls 207
Judgment, poor 68

K
Kinesthetic learner 36

L
Lack of awareness 68
Laws, family 202
Learner, kinesthetic 36
Learning 12
Learning actively 4
Learning from mistakes 156, 165
Learning to Bounce Back 156-179
Lectures 21, 26, 102
Lecturing parent 102
Level of expectations 39
Limitations 34
Limitations, intellectual 39
Limitations, physical 39
Limits 104
Listening actively 16
Logic 5, 27
Logical thinking 4, 157
Long-term goals 104, 114
Long-term objectives 96
Low self-esteem 41
Lying 102

M
Managing time 4
Manipulative behavior 40, 41
Marginal performance 130

Marginal preparation 130
Medium-range goals 114
Memory skills, visual 36
Mental health professionals 38
Metaphor 173
Mind, unconscious 34
Mind-set, negative 177
Mind-set, winner/loser 202
Mistakes, learning from 156, 165
Modification, behavior 68
Modifying the child's behavior 68
Monitoring system 83
Motivation 96

N
Natural ability 36
Natural resources 36
Negative associations 34, 177
Negative expectations 159
Negative experiences 34, 206
Negative mind-set 177
Negative reinforcement 133
Negotiable issues 202-203
Negotiation 41
Neutralizing 44
Non-achievement loop 101
Non-adaptive behavior 67
Non-communication 27
Non-judgmental tone 52
Non-logical answers 27
Non-negotiable family laws 202
Not-so-smart thinking 40
Nurturing, excessive 134

O
Objective assessment 195
Objectives 45
Objectives, long-term 96
Obligations 105
Obstacles 36, 157
Opinions 42
Oppression 101
Organizational Skills, Time
   Management and 129-155
Organizational skills 37, 129
Overcoming obstacles 36, 39

Ownership of the child's
  problem 48

P
Parent-child disagreements 202
Parent expectations 132
Parent talk 48
Parental self-restraint 115
Parents' prerogatives or
  authority 202
Participation, active 42, 102, 113
Passive resistance 102
Patience 22, 42
Payoffs 135
Perception, distortions in 177
Perceptiveness 37
Performance 118
Performance, marginal 130
Performance standards 38, 124
Performance, substandard 133
Periodic review of goals and
  achievements 121
Perseverance 124, 178
Personality 34
Perspective 34, 170
Persuasive arguments 206
Phobic behavior 37
Physical energy 34
Physical limitations 39
Physical survival 41
Planning, poor 68
Planning skills 37, 106
Planning strategically 10, 12
Poor judgment 68
Positive perspective 170
Potential abilities 12, 68, 117
Potential achievement 3
Potential, wasted 1
Power 144
Powerlessness 206
Practice 45
Praise 68, 69
Preparation, marginal 130
Prerogatives, parents' 202
Priorities and goals 4, 94-128
Prioritizing skills 153

Problem analysis 8
Problem-management checklist 75
Problem-solving and critical
  thinking skills 4
Problem-solving resources 44
Problem-solving skills 4
Problem-solving strategies 42
Problems, avoiding 40
Process of analysis 159
Process of error 159
Process of trial 159
Procrastination 102, 118, 129, 130
Procrastination/disorganization
  cycle 134
Proper instruction 35
Propulsion system 38
Protection 40
Protective behavior 34
Psychological barriers 177
Psychological imprinting 177
Psychological scarring 37
Psychological survival skills 41
Psychological turmoil 132
Punctuality 132
Punishment 68, 133
Purposeful introspection 71
Putting It All Together 180-208

R
Rationalization 41, 131
Reactionary behavior 139
Reactions, phobic 37
Reality 39
Reasoning deficiencies 27
Reasoning powers 27
Rebellion 102, 133
Reflexes 45, 60, 67
Reinforcement, negative 133
Reinforcements 68
Relevancy hooks 184
Remembering information 4
Rescuing 41, 133
Resentment 2, 5, 101
Resiliency 175
Resistance 5, 21, 41, 101, 102
Resolving conflicts 202

Resources, intellectual 11
Resources, natural 36
Resources, problem-solving 44
Response patterns 45
Responsibilities 105
Restraint 101
Reversals 167
Review of goals and
    achievements 121
Rewards 69, 106
Roadblocks 36
Role models 4
Rule-breaking 102
Rules 144

S
Sabotage 122
Sadness 2
Scarring, psychological 37
Schedule, study 144
School, struggling in 41
Security 40
Self-confidence 39, 70
Self-control 148
Self-defeating habits 131
Self-destructing 101
Self-discipline 102, 124
Self-doubt 118
Self-esteem 39, 41, 70
Self-examination 71
Self-restraint 94
Self-restraint, parental 115
Sensitivity 27
Sermons 21, 26
Setbacks 167
Short-term goals 114
Showdowns 144
Shutting down 27, 101, 159
Skills, analytical-thinking 183
Skills, deficient 12
Skills, organizational 37, 129
Skills, planning 37
Skills, prioritizing 153
Skills, problem-solving 4
Skills, psychological survival 41
Skills, strategic planning 106

Skills, strategic-thinking 37
Skills, visual memory 36
Smart thinking 8, 182
Smartness 8, 9
Smartness quotient 44
Solution-oriented thinking 157
Sorting principles 188
Stages, developmental 11
Standards of performance
    38, 124, 132
Stick-to-it-iveness 157, 177
Strategic decision-making 61
Strategic Introspection 64-93
Strategic planning 10, 12, 106
Strategic-thinking skills 4, 37
Strategies, communication 5, 15
Strategies, problem-solving 42
Strategy approach,
    examination/alternative 175
Stress 2, 159
Structure, external 148
Structure, internal 148
Structuring success 37
Struggling in school 41
Study schedule 144
Substandard performance 133
Success, structuring 37
Supercharging 38
Supportiveness 22
Survival mechanisms 167
Survival, financial 41
Survival, physical 41
Survival skills, psychological 41
Symbiotic relationship 133

T
Taking charge 68
Teasing 34
Teenagers 21
Tension, family 131
Thinking analytically 4, 7
Thinking logically 4
Thinking, not-so-smart 40
Thinking smart 8
Thinking, solution-oriented 157
Thinking strategically 4, 15

Thought, efficient 12
Thwarted adults 40
Thwarted children 40
Tightly knit families 13
Time Management and
    Organizational Skills 129-155
Time management 4
Time, inefficient use of 133
Time-efficient child 135
"Too-smart" child 90
Transformation 149
Trial, process of 104, 159
Trust 40, 48
Turmoil, psychological 132

U
Unconscious mind 34
Unconscious need 44
Underachievers 14

Underlying issues 27
Unrealistic expectations 115
Use of time, inefficient 133
Using goals for solving problems 4

V
Value system 117, 131-132
Victim role 68
Visual memory skills 36
Vulnerabilities 27, 34, 39, 176

W
Wasted potential 1
Weaknesses 34, 39
"Winner/loser" mind-set 202
Wise parents 139
Wise teachers 139
Work-together attitudes 48